by bob wiseman

southwest lite
full-flavored, healthy cooking

photography by
christopher marchetti

Northland Publishing

www.northlandbooks.com

Composed in the United States of America
Printed in China

Edited by Tammy Gales-Biber
Designed by Katie Jennings
Production supervised by Donna Boyd
Photography by Christopher Marchetti
Index by Jan Williams, Indexing Services

FIRST IMPRESSION 2005
ISBN 0-87358-878-9

05 06 07 08 09   5 4 3 2 1

Library of Congress Cataloging-in-Publication Data

Wiseman, Bob, 1937-
Southwest lite : full-flavored, healthy cooking / by Bob Wiseman.
p. cm.
Includes index.
1. Low-carbohydrate diet—Recipes. 2. Cookery, American—Southwestern style. I. Title.

RM237.73.W56 2005
641.5'6383—dc22
2004061663

Publisher's Note: The use of trade names does not imply an endorsement by the product manufacturer. Nutritional analysis compiled using MasterCook 7 software. All figures are complete and accurate to the best of our knowledge.

I gratefully dedicate this cookbook to my good friends
Robert Shiroff, MD; D. Craig Miller, MD; and Robert Wiencek, Jr., MD.
No one could ask for better friends at the poker game of life.

contents

foreword

by Dave DeWitt

Because the press has dubbed me "The Pope of Peppers," I was more than happy to be asked to write the foreword for Bob Wiseman's new hot and spicy Southwest cookbook. The first thing I examined was Bob's use of chiles, and I wasn't disappointed. Although the hot stuff isn't part of every single recipe, there are enough spicy dishes to satisfy any chile-head. But chiles are only one of the authentic flavors of the Southwest, and Bob gives us plenty more with dishes infused with cilantro, Mexican oregano, tomatillos, salsa, epazote, pecans, and good-old dark Mexican beer.

The concept of this book fits in with today's ingredient-conscious cooks, and Bob freely uses substitutes for sugar, salt, and fat. And far from being overly serious, he has fun with the recipes, using innovative titles like Hawaiian Cowboy Salsa, Rainbow Pasta Salad, and Gadzooks! It's Clam Gazpacho. This book is packed full of imaginative recipes like Scallion-Cilantro Sauce, Eggplant Sonora with Wild Rice, Focaccia with a Southwestern Twist, and Buttermilk Meatloaf. I can't wait to use his truly unique Hot August Night Barbecue Sauce, and I like Bob's take on chicken-fried steak, which he dubs Pecan Crusted Cowboy-Style Steak with Mushroom Milk Gravy.

The nutritional information accompanying each recipe is useful for dieters and people watching their salt and sugar intake. Now, thanks to Bob Wiseman, people on any diet can enjoy the delicious flavors of the region with *Southwest Lite: Full-flavored, Healthy Cooking*.

introduction

My first low-fat, low-sodium southwestern cookbook, *Healthy Southwestern Cooking* by Northland Publishing, was brought about by a doctor who found a problem with a valve in my heart. He handed me a piece of paper detailing a bland diet and, wagging a finger at me, stated that I had to cut down on the salt and fat. Well, little did he know that I wasn't about to give up the zesty flavors of the Southwest. I had been at the stove and over countless campfires way too long to change my diet. There had to be a better way.

I had been cooking long enough to know how to substitute one item for another, so it wasn't too hard for me to come up with a saddlebag full of low-sodium, low-fat Tex-Mex recipes that were still as tasty as the originals. Soon my kitchen was up and running, and tasty, spicy Southwest cuisine was still alive on my kitchen table. And, most importantly, the nutritional factors of the revamped recipes fit right in with the diet I had been ordered to follow. The wise old doctor didn't know it at the time, but he had inspired a cookbook.

This spring I was chatting with Northland about a new cookbook, and they asked if I could come up with another healthy Southwest cookbook. So I mixed and matched the basic philosophies of all of today's popular diets with some old-fashioned common sense and came up with a selection of recipes that will appeal to everyone who loves the spicy flavors of the Southwest.

All of the nutritional facts found in this book were calculated on a 2000-calorie-per-day diet, and I've tried to keep the ingredients simple. I do use a handful of brand names throughout the book, because that's what I use in my kitchen. But the products are, in most cases, available in their name brand form as well as a generic form almost everywhere throughout the United States, Mexico, and Canada. And, if you can't find what you need, then check the listing of mail order sources in the back of the book.

So now it's your chance to try a new style of flavorful cooking with *Southwest Lite*. Open any page; select a healthy, heart-smart recipe; and start cooking today!

appetizers

camarones especiales

The Gulf of Mexico and the Gulf of California are rich with shrimp, and a fresh batch of this shrimp salsa is the perfect dip to offer at a brunch or pool-side party. I serve it with salt-free tortilla chips or toast triangles.

8 ounces Neufchatel cheese
1/2 cup Mock Sour Cream
   (see recipe on page 97)
1/2 teaspoon balsamic vinegar
1 teaspoon hot sauce, El Pato preferred
1 tablespoon olive oil
1 clove garlic, finely minced
1/2 teaspoon salt substitute
1/4 teaspoon ground cumin
1/2 cup finely minced red bell pepper
1/2 cup finely minced green bell pepper
1/4 cup minced scallions
1 cup shrimp, cooked and minced
Fresh cilantro

Bring all ingredients to room temperature, except the shrimp, which is to be kept chilled.

   Combine all ingredients, except the cilantro, in a deep bowl and blend thoroughly. Garnish with the cilantro. Refrigerate for at least 1 hour to allow flavors to blend.

Makes 3 1/2 Cups, about 36 Servings

nutritional facts
per serving

Calories 30
Total Fat 2g
Cholesterol 18mg
Sodium 54mg
Total Carbohydrate 1g
Dietary Fiber *trace*
Protein 2g

devil's kisses

If you like the flavorful blast of chipotle chiles, then you'll love these little zingers. Just take a bite and wait a few moments... Suddenly, the sneaky punch hits you with a pleasing, spicy tang. For a spicier flavor, you can add another chipotle. Be cautious, though, as chipotles pack a wallop.

1/2 cup Shedd's Spread Country Crock, softened
2 cups shredded Cheddar cheese
2 chipotle chiles in adobo sauce, minced
1/2 cup all-purpose flour
1/4 teaspoon salt substitute
1/4 teaspoon ground cumin
2 tablespoons cold water
1/4 teaspoon mesquite flavoring, optional

To make the cracker dough, add the Shedd's Spread, cheese, and chipotle to a blender or food processor and mix well. Add the flour, salt, cumin, water, and, if desired, mesquite flavoring, and blend just until mixed. Wrap the dough in plastic wrap, and refrigerate for 30 minutes to firm the dough.

Preheat the oven to 325°F. Spray a cookie sheet with vegetable spray. Roll the dough into 1-inch balls and place on the cookie sheet. Bake for 15 to 20 minutes, or until lightly browned. Cool on a rack, and serve immediately. These zesty crackers will store for up to 1 week in an air-tight container.

Makes 48 Crackers, about 24 Servings

nutritional facts
per serving

Calories 25
Total Fat 2g
Cholesterol 4mg
Sodium 34mg
Total Carbohydrate 1g
Dietary Fiber trace
Protein 1g

little firecrackers

If you want to get the party started, then put out a bowl of Little Firecrackers. I guarantee these spicy nuts will get everyone's attention, so make sure you have plenty of cold beer handy. If you want the nuts a little hotter, kick up the heat with a little cayenne powder or powdered jalapeño. These hot nuts can be stored for up to 1 month, but I've never had a jar that lasted longer than a day or so—they are just too tempting.

1 cup dry-roasted peanuts
1 cup almonds
1 cup pecans
1 cup hazelnuts
1 teaspoon sesame seeds
1 teaspoon egg substitute
1/4 teaspoon salt substitute
1/4 teaspoon garlic powder
1 teaspoon Tabasco, or your favorite hot sauce
1 teaspoon canola oil

Preheat the oven to 250°F. Add all ingredients, including extra chile powder, if desired, to a deep bowl and mix well to coat. Spread the coated nuts evenly on a cookie sheet and bake for 15 minutes. Drain the nuts on paper towels and let cool. Place in a bowl and serve immediately. Store any excess in an air-tight container in a cool, dry place.

Makes 4 Cups, about 36 Servings

nutritional facts
per serving

Calories 95
Total Fat 9g
Cholesterol trace
Sodium 36mg
Total Carbohydrate 3g
Dietary Fiber 1g
Protein 2g

cisco's bagel bites

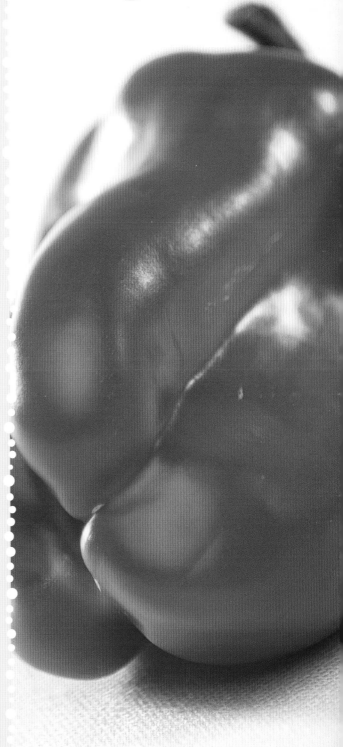

Jalapeño bagels are available at most supermarket deli counters and bakeries. Spread this delicious cheese mix on the bagels and suddenly you'll have a tasty, appealing snack.

    8 ounces Neufchatel cheese
    1 cup Salsa Numero Uno
      (see recipe on page 17)
    8 jalapeño bagels
    1 tablespoon chopped fresh cilantro leaves

Warm the cream cheese in a microwave until soft, about 15 seconds. In a deep bowl, mix together the warm cheese and the Salsa Numero Uno, blending thoroughly. Split the bagels in half, toast them, and generously spread the cheese and salsa mixture on each half. Garnish each bagel half with cilantro. Cut the topped bagels in quarters, place on a tray, and serve as an appetizer.

Makes about 16 Servings

nutritional facts
per serving

Calories 167
Total Fat 4g
Cholesterol 11mg
Sodium 341mg
Total Carbohydrate 26g
Dietary Fiber 1g
Protein 6g

create-your-own potato skins

These tasty potato skins are not recommended for those on a strict low-carb diet, but they will be a welcome addition to your party, brunch, or other special occasion. Make sure to have all of your topping choices handy as soon as the stuffed skins come out of the oven.

> 2 tablespoons Shedd's Spread Country Crock, room temperature
> 1 tablespoon salt substitute
> 12 red potatoes, washed and scrubbed
> 1 cup shredded mozzarella cheese
> 1 cup low-fat mayonnaise
> 1 tablespoon paprika
> 1 medium red onion, minced

Preheat the oven to 400°F. Mix the Shedd's Spread and salt substitute to make a paste. Roll the potatoes in the paste to coat. Bake for 1 hour, or until the potatoes pierce easily with a skewer or toothpick. Remove and let cool for 15 to 20 minutes. Slice the potatoes in half the long way, carefully scoop out the pulp, and save the pulp for other uses.

In a bowl, combine the mozzarella, mayonnaise, paprika, and onion and mix well. Spoon even amounts of the cheese mixture into the potato skins. Bake until the cheese mix is bubbly, about 3 to 4 minutes. Allow to cool slightly before topping.

Arrange various dishes of chopped tomatoes, scallions, imitation bacon bits, Mock Sour Cream (see recipe on page 97), hot sauce, salsa, or any other topping you might like to use. Let your guests top off their own skins with their favorite ingredients.

Makes 24 Servings

nutritional facts
per serving

Calories 78
Total Fat 4g
Cholesterol 8mg
Sodium 76mg
Total Carbohydrate 8g
Dietary Fiber 1g
Protein 2g

carlos the clam dip

This dip is a crowd pleaser at my house, and it's the perfect appetizer for New Year's Eve parties and Super Bowl gatherings. Keep an eye on this cookbook or your guests will steal the recipe page from you. Serve with sliced vegetables, tortilla chips, or wheat crackers.

6 1/2 ounces chopped clams with juice
3 large garlic cloves, minced
2 pickled jalapeño chiles, finely minced
8 ounces Neufchatel cheese
4 ounces shredded mozzarella cheese
1 tablespoon minced fresh basil
1/2 teaspoon ground ginger
1 teaspoon minced capers
1/2 teaspoon salt substitute
1/4 cup low-fat mayonnaise
1/2 cup shredded Romano cheese

Preheat the oven to 350°F. In a square 8 x 8-inch casserole dish, combine the clams, garlic, jalapeños, Neufchatel cheese, mozzarella cheese, basil, ginger, capers, salt, and mayonnaise. Mix to blend. Sprinkle the Romano cheese on top of the mix. Bake until lightly browned and bubbly, about 20 to 25 minutes. Remove from the oven and let cool for 10 minutes. Serve warm.

Makes 3 1/2 Cups, about 24 Servings

nutritional facts
per serving

Calories 67
Total Fat 5*g*
Cholesterol 20*mg*
Sodium 110*mg*
Total Carbohydrate 1*g*
Dietary Fiber *trace*
Protein 5*g*

festival spread

Now here is a colorful spread that is far superior to the spreads served on dinky little toast pieces or brittle wheat crackers. I use my Festival Spread as a filling for omelets, enchiladas, tacos, or just about any recipe that calls for a stuffing. For a quick snack or appetizer, fill Portobello mushrooms with Festival Spread, top them with shredded Cheddar cheese, and then broil them until the cheese has melted. Now you have a real treat.

1/2 cup low-fat cottage cheese
8 ounces Neufchatel cheese
1/2 stalk celery, chopped
1 small carrot, chopped
1/2 cup chopped red bell pepper
1/4 cup diced green chiles
1/4 cup diced onion
1/2 teaspoon Old Bay Seasoning
1/4 teaspoon celery seeds
3 drops vanilla extract

Combine all ingredients in a food processor and blend until nicely chopped. Place in a decorative bowl, and serve immediately. This spread will store well in an air-tight container in the refrigerator for up to 2 weeks.

Makes 2 1/2 Cups, about 20 Servings

nutritional facts
per serving

Calories 38
Total Fat 3g
Cholesterol 9mg
Sodium 87mg
Total Carbohydrate 1g
Dietary Fiber *trace*
Protein 2g

paco's shrimp and creamy mango dip

This tasty appetizer can be used as a filling for omelets or wrapped in flour tortillas and then chilled and cut into rounds. I quarter Little Corn Tortillas (see recipe on page 100) and use the "chips" for dipping, or, if you prefer, you can use pita bread pieces with this appetizer. For a spicier dip add an extra minced serrano chile or kick it up with your favorite hot sauce.

1/2 cup chopped red bell pepper
8 ounces Neufchatel cheese
1/2 cup low-fat cottage cheese
1 scallion, chopped
2 tablespoons low-fat evaporated milk
1 teaspoon salt substitute
2 tablespoons minced ginger
1 small jalapeño chile or serrano chile
30 medium shrimp, cooked and
   coarsely chopped
2 mangoes, peeled and coarsely chopped
1/2 cup chopped fresh cilantro

In a blender, combine the red bell pepper, Neufchatel cheese, cottage cheese, scallion, evaporated milk, salt substitute, ginger, and jalapeño or serrano. Blend until smooth. Fold in the shrimp, mango, and cilantro. Refrigerate for 1 hour or longer. Serve immediately.

Makes 3 1/2 Cups, about 40 Servings

nutritional facts
per serving

Calories 14
Total Fat 1g
Cholesterol 8mg
Sodium 22mg
Total Carbohydrate 1g
Dietary Fiber trace
Protein 1g

salsas

hawaiian cowboy salsa

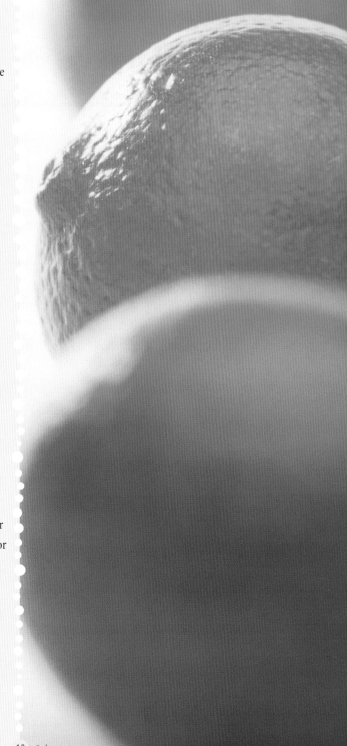

The largest ranch in the United States is on the Big Island of Hawaii. Tending to the cows are paniolos, the name given to Hawaiian cowboys. This salsa combines the spicy spirit of the Southwest with the rich flavors of the Pacific Rim.

3 Roma tomatoes, diced
1/2 cup chopped white onion
1 tangerine, skinned and diced
1/4 cup finely chopped cashews
1/4 cup finely chopped macadamia nuts
3/4 cup minced watercress
1/2 teaspoon lemon grass herb
   blend, optional
1 slice fresh ginger, finely minced
1 tablespoon minced scallions
1/2 cup diced green chiles
1 serrano chile, minced
1 teaspoon El Pato hot sauce
1/4 teaspoon chili powder
1/4 teaspoon salt substitute
1 teaspoon canola oil
1/2 teaspoon rice wine vinegar,
   or red wine vinegar
1 teaspoon fresh lime juice

Combine all ingredients in a bowl, and mix thoroughly. Cover and refrigerate for 1 hour. Serve over grilled chicken or fish or with fresh tortilla chips.

Makes 3 Cups, about 24 Servings

nutritional facts
per serving

Calories 28
Total Fat 2g
Cholesterol *trace*
Sodium 10mg
Total Carbohydrate 3g
Dietary Fiber 1g
Protein 1g

roasted green tomato salsa

My tomatoes grew to size, turned slightly yellow, and formed orange and red streaks down the sides. They did everything but turn solid red. They appeared to be just short of fully ripening. The variegated coloring was appealing, but the flavor for the table wasn't quite right, so I decided to convert them into a salsa. The final results yielded a slightly tart but refreshing salsa. The addition of fresh basil rather than cilantro adds a nice touch. This salsa can also be used as a sauce over chicken breasts, pork chops, or red snapper filets.

2 1/2 tablespoons extra virgin olive oil
6 green tomatoes, quartered
1 green bell pepper, quartered
1/4 teaspoon salt substitute
Dash black pepper
1/4 teaspoon granulated garlic
3 cloves garlic, minced
1 (4-ounce) can chopped green chiles
2 scallions, minced
1/4 teaspoon chili powder
1 teaspoon dried oregano, the Mexican
    variety preferred
2 tablespoons minced fresh cilantro
1/2 teaspoon ground cumin
1/4 teaspoon Tabasco, or other hot sauce
1 teaspoon lemon juice
1 teaspoon minced fresh basil leaves

Preheat the oven to 350° F. Coat the bottom of an 8 x 8-inch baking dish with the olive oil. Add the tomatoes and bell pepper, and roll in the oil to coat. Sprinkle the salt, pepper, and garlic on the mixture. Bake in the oven for 30 minutes, turn the mixture in the dish, and bake for another 15 minutes. Remove the dish, cool, and then cover with foil or plastic wrap and refrigerate for at least 1 hour.

With a paring knife, carefully remove the skin from the tomatoes and bell peppers and gently squeeze the juices from them. Dice or chop the mix and set aside. Add the remaining ingredients and refrigerate for at least 1 hour. Adjust the seasoning to taste, and serve with tortilla chips.

Makes 5 Cups, about 40 Servings

nutritional facts
per serving

Calories 17
Total Fat 1g
Cholesterol *trace*
Sodium 4mg
Total Carbohydrate 2g
Dietary Fiber *trace*
Protein *trace*

salsa pico

This salsa can be thrown together in a hurry. The contents are best if they are garden fresh.

3 small green tomatoes, chopped
2 small red or green bell peppers, chopped
1/4 cup chopped red onion
1/2 cup chopped green chiles
1/8 teaspoon cilantro powder (see recipe on page 95)
1/4 teaspoon extra virgin olive oil
1/2 teaspoon fresh lemon juice
1/8 teaspoon dried oregano, the Mexican variety preferred
1/8 teaspoon El Pato hot sauce
Dash salt substitute

Combine all ingredients in a deep bowl and mix well. Cover and refrigerate for at least 1 hour before serving. Serve with fresh, chopped vegetables.

Makes 3 Cups, about 24 Servings

nutritional facts
per serving

Calories 11
Total Fat *trace*
Cholesterol 0*mg*
Sodium 4*mg*
Total Carbohydrate 2*g*
Dietary Fiber 1*g*
Protein *trace*

salsa supreme

This is my version of the puréed red sauce found on tables at Mexican restaurants. To give it a real kick, add a minced chipotle chile or a hearty dash of habanero powder.

9 Roma tomatoes, coarsely chopped
1 cup chopped white onion
1 cup diced green chiles
2 small serrano chiles, minced
1 small jalapeño chile, minced
1/4 cup minced fresh cilantro
3 cloves garlic, minced
1/2 tablespoon balsamic vinegar
1 teaspoon canola oil
2 teaspoons fresh lemon juice
1/4 teaspoon salt substitute
1 tablespoon salsa seasoning, or Texas Jack's Seasoning (see recipe on page 89)

Combine all ingredients in a blender and mix until puréed. Strain to remove particles. Cover and refrigerate for at least 1 hour before serving. Serve with your favorite tortilla chips.

Makes 5 Cups, about 40 Servings

nutritional facts
per serving

Calories 12
Total Fat *trace*
Cholesterol *trace*
Sodium 42*mg*
Total Carbohydrate 2*g*
Dietary Fiber *trace*
Protein *trace*

salsa canada

In the summer of 2003, I was part of a rag-tag crew shuttling a large yacht from Marina del Rey, California, to Vancouver, British Columbia. We had to clear Canadian customs at a port on a small island. While waiting, I whipped up this salsa from ingredients in the galley. It was a pleasant evening watching the sun set, drinking Canadian beer, and enjoying this spicy salsa.

1 large tomato, chopped
1/4 teaspoon garlic powder
1/4 teaspoon chili powder
1/8 teaspoon ground cumin
1 tablespoon shredded Parmesan cheese
1/4 cup minced red onion
1 jalapeño chile, minced
1 large tangerine, chopped
2 scallions, minced
Dash salt substitute
1/2 teaspoon chili sauce, Caravelle
    Thai-style preferred
1 teaspoon balsamic vinegar
1/2 teaspoon extra virgin olive oil
Dash hot sauce

Mix all ingredients in a medium bowl, cover, and refrigerate for at least 1 hour. Serve immediately with your favorite tortilla chips.

Makes 2 Cups, about 16 Servings

nutritional facts
per serving

Calories *7*
Total Fat *trace*
Cholesterol *trace*
Sodium *7mg*
Total Carbohydrate *trace*
Dietary Fiber *trace*
Protein *trace*

salsa numero uno

This salsa is similar to most classic salsas, but I've added a few extra ingredients to kick it up a little.

4 Roma tomatoes, seeded and diced
1/4 cup diced red bell pepper
1/4 cup diced green bell pepper
1/2 cup diced yellow bell pepper
3 cloves garlic, minced
1/2 cup diced white onions
3 scallions, minced
1/4 cup minced fresh cilantro
1 tablespoon fresh lime juice
1/8 teaspoon salt substitute
1/4 cup Herdez Salsa Verde
1 teaspoon canola oil
1/4 teaspoon ground cumin
1/8 teaspoon chili powder
1 teaspoon dried oregano, the Mexican
  variety preferred
1/2 teaspoon cilantro powder (see recipe
  on page 95)
1 teaspoon Tabasco, or your favorite hot sauce
1 teaspoon rice vinegar
1/4 teaspoon Splenda sugar substitute

Combine all ingredients in a large bowl and mix thoroughly. Cover and refrigerate for at least 1 hour. Serve with tortilla chips, pita slices, or fresh vegetables.

Makes 3 1/2 Cups, about 28 Servings

nutritional facts
per serving

Calories 14
Total Fat *trace*
Cholesterol *0mg*
Sodium *79mg*
Total Carbohydrate *3g*
Dietary Fiber *trace*
Protein *trace*

the new bernstein salsa

Al Bernstein, the noted boxing critic, is a friend of mine. Every time I'm invited to appear on his Las Vegas radio program, I'll blend up a new batch of this salsa and take it to him. It packs a real punch, and, as Al claims, "this salsa takes no prisoners."

1 (14-ounce) can diced tomatoes with
    green chiles
1/2 cup minced white onion
4 green chiles, roasted, peeled, and
    coarsely chopped
1/2 cup chopped red bell pepper
1/4 cup chopped scallions
1/2 cup green taco sauce
1/4 cup minced fresh cilantro
1 teaspoon fresh lime juice
2 teaspoons habanero hot sauce, or the
    hottest you have
1/8 teaspoon Splenda sugar substitute
1 tablespoon salsa seasoning, or Texas
    Jack's Seasoning (see recipe on page 89)
1/8 teaspoon granulated garlic
Dash salt substitute

Combine all ingredients in a large bowl. Cover and refrigerate for at least 2 hours or overnight. Serve and enjoy!

Makes 4 1/2 Cups, about 36 Servings

nutritional facts
per serving

Calories 12
Total Fat *trace*
Cholesterol *trace*
Sodium *42mg*
Total Carbohydrate *2g*
Dietary Fiber *trace*
Protein *trace*

soups and stews

gadzooks! it's clam gazpacho

Here's a summer soup that is served cold right from the refrigerator. You might say it is the Southwest's answer to the East Coast soup, Manhattan Chowder. Have the hot sauce handy at the table so your family and guests can spice it up the way they like it.

1 quart clam and tomato juice,
   Clamato preferred
1/2 cup chopped zucchini
1/2 cup chopped scallions
1/2 cup minced water chestnuts
1 small cucumber, diced
1 avocado, peeled, pitted, and diced
1/2 cup diced celery
1/2 cup crumbled feta cheese
1 tablespoon hot sauce, Gadzooks! preferred
1/2 teaspoon ground celery seeds
1/2 teaspoon cracked black pepper
1 teaspoon mild chili powder
1/4 cup chopped fresh cilantro

Combine all ingredients, except the fresh cilantro, in a glass or plastic bowl; cover and refrigerate for at least 4 hours. Garnish with chopped cilantro, and serve chilled.

Makes 12 Small Servings

nutritional facts
per serving

Calories 143
Total Fat 6g
Cholesterol 8mg
Sodium 658mg
Total Carbohydrate 20g
Dietary Fiber 2g
Protein 3g

garlic bread caldito

Here's a spicy Basque sheepherder soup that's outstanding and as old as the hills of the Basque region of northern Spain and southwestern France. Garlic bread and spicy soup have been staples in the Basque diet for centuries and are common fare at most Basque restaurants. I suggest you serve this soup with a hearty Burgundy wine.

1 loaf French bread
1/2 cup extra virgin olive oil
8 garlic cloves, mashed
1 teaspoon paprika
1/4 teaspoon hot chili powder, or to taste
1/4 teaspoon salt substitute
2 cups Low-Sodium Chicken Stock
   (see recipe on page 89)
1 cup egg substitute

Cut the French bread into thick slices and allow to dry on each side, about 15 minutes per side.

Heat a Dutch oven or heavy, deep skillet until a drop of water quickly sizzles away. Add the olive oil and mashed garlic and brown lightly on both sides. Add the dried bread slices.

In a separate small bowl, mix the paprika, hot chili powder, and salt substitute with 2 tablespoons of water. Pour over the bread. Add the chicken stock. Bring to a simmer, keeping the heat on low. Simmer for 30 minutes, adding just enough water to keep the bread covered. Just before serving, whisk the egg substitute into the soup. Serve at once.

Makes 6 Servings

nutritional facts
per serving

Calories 454
Total Fat 25g
Cholesterol 1mg
Sodium 715mg
Total Carbohydrate 43g
Dietary Fiber 2g
Protein 15g

grilled pork rib caldo

What a treat this stew is. The flavor of the grilled ribs adds a nice touch, and the stringy mozzarella offers a pleasing, chewy texture. If you want to spice up the soup, add a few drops of your favorite hot sauce and smoky mesquite or hickory flavoring. Serve it as hot as you can handle it!

- 4 large pre-grilled country-style pork ribs
- 1 teaspoon horseradish
- 2 cups Low-Sodium Chicken Stock
  (see recipe on page 89)
- 1/4 teaspoon garlic powder
- 1 cup minced white onion
- 8 slices mozzarella cheese
- Strips of corn tortillas
- Fresh parsley or cilantro

Remove the meat from the ribs, reserve the bones, and then cube the meat in 1/2-inch pieces. In a large soup pot, combine the meat, bones, horseradish, chicken stock, garlic powder, and onion. Bring to a boil and then reduce to a simmer.

Let cook for 45 minutes, remove the bones, and refrigerate the soup for 1 hour to set the flavors. Bring back to a simmer and heat through. Line each soup bowl with mozzarella slices, and add the hot soup. Garnish with a handful of tortilla strips and a few sprigs of fresh parsley or cilantro.

Makes 4-6 Servings

nutritional facts
Per Serving

Calories 274
Total Fat 20g
Cholesterol 73mg
Sodium 364mg
Total Carbohydrate 4g
Dietary Fiber 1g
Protein 22g

chile verde

Chile Verde is the flagship dish of New Mexico. No matter where you go, it's on the menu. And I guarantee that each bowl of Chile Verde will taste different at every location, from mild to hot to hottest. This particular recipe is similar to the one my wife and I use in competition chili cook-offs, and we have qualified twice to compete in the International Chili Society World Championship.

1 tablespoon canola oil

2 1/2 pounds pork loin, fat trimmed off and cubed

1/2 pound Mojave Sausage (see recipe on page 53)

6 cloves garlic, minced

2 medium onions, diced

1/4 cup diced green bell pepper

1 bay leaf

8 ounces Herdez Salsa Verde

1 1/2 cups chopped roasted green chiles

1 cup green enchilada sauce

2 cups Low-Sodium Chicken Stock (see recipe on page 89)

1 teaspoon dried oregano, the Mexican variety preferred

1 tablespoon ground cumin

2 teaspoons salt substitute

Cayenne or jalapeño powder, to taste

Heat a skillet or Dutch oven until a drop of water quickly sizzles away, and then add the canola oil. Brown the pork cubes and Mojave Sausage in batches, putting each batch aside in the pot you intend to use for the stew. Drain off all but 2 tablespoons of the pork drippings, and add the garlic, onion, and bell pepper. Sauté for 2 to 3 minutes, or until lightly browned. To the pot with the browned pork and sausage, add the sautéed vegetables, bay leaf, salsa verde, green chiles, enchilada sauce, chicken stock, oregano, cumin, and salt substitute. Bring to a boil, and then reduce to a simmer; cook for 30 minutes.

After 30 minutes, check stew for taste. If needed, add extra cumin 1/2 teaspoon at a time. Add water if the broth is too thick; you should have about 1/2 inch of broth over the stew. Simmer for 30 more minutes and then taste again. Cover the pot, turn off the stove, and let the stew rest for 1 full hour. Taste again when it's cool, and add cayenne or jalapeño powder to suit your taste.

Turn the burner back on, bring the stew to a simmer, and adjust for flavor one last time. Serve with a dab of sour cream and flour tortillas or corn bread on the side.

Makes 12 Small Servings

nutritional facts
per serving

Calories 204
Total Fat 11g
Cholesterol 53mg
Sodium 272mg
Total Carbohydrate 7g
Dietary Fiber 1g
Protein 20g

ham and a pair of beans stew

If you have a leftover ham bone, this is where to use it. Add a hearty side of cornbread and a nice salad, and you'll have a tasty meal.

3 cups Low-Sodium Chicken Stock
(see recipe on page 89)
3 cups Low-Sodium Beef Stock
(see recipe on page 87)
1 1/2 cups light beer, at room temperature
1 (1/4-ounce) package onion soup mix
1 teaspoon Old Bay Seasoning, or
Cajun seasoning
1 bay leaf
3/4 cup black-eyed peas, washed
and sorted
3/4 cup great Northern beans, washed
and sorted
1/2 cup chopped red or green bell peppers
2 cloves garlic, minced
1 ham bone, with some meat
1/2 teaspoon salt substitute

In a deep stew pot or Dutch oven, bring both broths and the beer to a boil. Add the remaining ingredients and let boil for 30 minutes. Reduce to a simmer, cover, and let cook for 2 to 3 hours, or until the beans are cooked through. Remove the meat from the ham bone, discard the ham bone, and add the meat back to the pot. Heat for approximately 5 more minutes, and serve hot in deep bowls.

Makes 12 Small Servings

nutritional facts
per serving

Calories 211
Total Fat 10g
Cholesterol 28mg
Sodium 484mg
Total Carbohydrate 17g
Dietary Fiber 4g
Protein 15g

el paso albóndigas soup

Here's a great recipe that's served all over the Southwest. I use my own Spiced Veal Meatballs (see recipe on page 52) with this soup.

- 1 quart Low-Sodium Chicken Stock (see recipe on page 89)
- 2 cans El Pato tomato sauce
- 6 ounces Mexican beer
- 12 cooked meatballs, or Spiced Veal Meatballs
- 1/4 cup shredded carrots
- 1/4 cup minced onion
- 1/4 cup shredded Parmesan cheese
- 1/4 teaspoon salt substitute
- 1/4 teaspoon hot sauce

Combine all ingredients in a deep stew pot or Dutch oven. Bring to a boil, reduce to a simmer, and then cook for 15 to 20 minutes. Serve immediately with Bandito Bolillos (see recipe on page 101).

Makes 6 Servings

nutritional facts
per serving

Calories 150
Total Fat 8g
Cholesterol 13mg
Sodium 658mg
Total Carbohydrate 5g
Dietary Fiber 1g
Protein 13g

gazpacho grande

This cold soup is typical of the traditional Spanish-style gazpacho. Sometimes I'll float a dab of Mock Sour Cream (see recipe on page 97) on each serving of the gazpacho and adorn it with a large cooked shrimp.

2 cups diced tomatoes
1/2 cup diced green chiles
1/4 cup chopped watercress
1 cup diced cucumber
1/2 cup diced red bell pepper
1 cup diced celery
2 scallions, minced
6 oyster mushrooms, chopped
1/2 cup green taco sauce,
    La Victoria preferred
1 cup Herdez Salsa Verde
1 teaspoon hot sauce
1/4 teaspoon granulated garlic
1/8 teaspoon salt substitute
1/4 teaspoon mild chili powder
3 cups clam and tomato juice,
    Clamato preferred
Lemon wedges

Mix all ingredients in a glass or plastic container. Cover and refrigerate for at least 2 hours. Serve chilled with lemon wedges on the side.

Makes 12 Small Servings

nutritional facts
per serving

Calories 80
Total Fat 1g
Cholesterol *trace*
Sodium 394mg
Total Carbohydrate 16g
Dietary Fiber 3g
Protein 4g

salads

april on the patio potato salad

I call this easy-to-make dish April on the Patio Potato Salad, because that is the perfect way to serve it. The fresh dill and chives I grow on my patio really make a tasty difference in this springtime salad.

3 cups boiled potatoes, cut in $1/2$-inch
  thick cubes
$1/2$ cup low-fat French dressing
$1/4$ cup egg substitute, hard-cooked
  and chopped
1 teaspoon minced fresh dill
$1/4$ cup chopped red bell pepper
1 clove garlic, minced
1 teaspoon minced fresh chives
Dash white pepper
Dash salt substitute

Combine all ingredients in a deep bowl and gently stir until mixed. Refrigerate for 1 hour before serving. Sit out on the patio and enjoy!

Makes 4-6 Servings

nutritional facts
per serving

Calories 104
Total Fat 2g
Cholesterol 37mg
Sodium 184mg
Total Carbohydrate 19g
Dietary Fiber 1g
Protein 2g

artichoke and leek salad

Artichokes in oil are a mainstay in my kitchen. When I need a quick salad, I look for them in the pantry. The shrimp and feta cheese add a tasty, appealing flavor.

  4 cups chopped romaine lettuce
  4 thin slices red bell pepper
  1/4 cup egg substitute, hard-cooked
    and chopped
  4 medium shrimp, cooked and coarsely chopped
  1 small leek, cut in 1/2-inch rounds
  4 artichoke bottoms, cubed
  1/4 cup crumbled feta cheese
  2 small radishes, finely chopped
  4 tablespoons Five Flavors Sauce
    (see recipe on page 92)

Arrange equal portions of romaine in chilled salad bowls. Place the red bell pepper slices in the middle. Sprinkle the chopped egg substitute and shrimp around the outside edges of the bowl. Arrange the leek rounds next to the bell pepper. Place an artichoke bottom in the center of the bell pepper. Sprinkle the feta cheese and radishes over the artichoke. Drizzle the Five Flavors Sauce over the salad. Serve immediately.

Makes 4 Servings

nutritional facts
per serving

Calories 148
Total Fat 4g
Cholesterol 65mg
Sodium 675mg
Total Carbohydrate 20g
Dietary Fiber 7g
Protein 9g

curried tuna salad

Curry and tuna are a unique pair—a combination you will find very tasty. This low-carb salad is great when served on a crisp romaine leaf.

- 2 (4-ounce) cans albacore
- 2 tablespoons low-fat cottage cheese
- 2 tablespoons Mock Sour Cream (see recipe on page 97)
- 1/2 cup low-fat mayonnaise
- 1 tablespoon minced onion
- 1 medium tomato, chopped and seeded
- 1 stalk celery, diced
- 1/2 cup diced cucumber
- 1/4 cup egg substitute, hard-cooked and chopped
- 1/8 teaspoon onion powder
- 1/8 teaspoon garlic powder
- 1/4 teaspoon curry powder
- 1/8 teaspoon El Pato hot sauce
- Salt and pepper, to taste

Combine all ingredients in a large bowl and mix thoroughly. Refrigerate for at least 1 hour to allow the flavors to blend. Serve chilled over a crisp leaf of romaine lettuce, if desired.

Makes 8 Servings

nutritional facts
per serving

Calories 98
Total Fat 5g
Cholesterol 40mg
Sodium 222mg
Total Carbohydrate 3g
Dietary Fiber *trace*
Protein 9g

chile and bean salad

Here's a simple green bean salad, which you can also use as a side dish. It is also the perfect salad to bring on picnics.

14 ounces fresh green beans
1 (4-ounce) can diced green chiles
1/4 cup chopped red onion
1/4 cup rice vinegar
1/4 teaspoon salt substitute
1/2 teaspoon Splenda sugar substitute
1/2 teaspoon caraway seeds

Combine all ingredients in a deep bowl and mix thoroughly. Refrigerate for 1 hour before serving.

Makes 4-6 Servings

nutritional facts
per serving

Calories 28
Total Fat *trace*
Cholesterol *trace*
Sodium *5mg*
Total Carbohydrate *7g*
Dietary Fiber *2g*
Protein *1g*

holiday salad

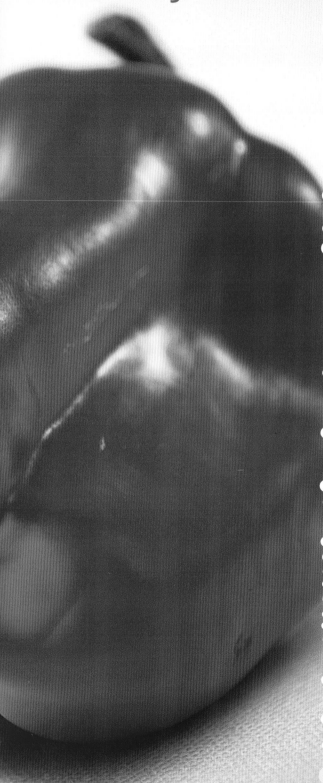

No matter what time of year, this salad is a favorite with our guests and family. It is easy to make and full of flavor.

3 cups cooked and diced red potatoes
1/2 cup chopped white onion
1/2 cup diced cucumber
3 scallions, minced
1/4 cup chopped red or green bell pepper
1/4 cup raisins
1 small Granny Smith apple, diced
3/4 cup egg substitute, hard-cooked
   and chopped
1/4 teaspoon salt substitute
1/4 teaspoon Colman's English
   Mustard powder
1/4 teaspoon Old Bay Seasoning
1/4 teaspoon cracked black pepper
1/2 teaspoon celery seeds
1/2 cup low-fat mayonnaise
2 sprigs fresh basil, minced

Mix all ingredients together in a large bowl and refrigerate for at least 1 hour. Serve chilled for any occasion.

Makes 4-6 Servings

nutritional facts
per serving

Calories 186
Total Fat 8g
Cholesterol 100mg
Sodium 156mg
Total Carbohydrate 25g
Dietary Fiber 3g
Protein 5g

macaroni salad mexicana

Epazote is a common herb in the Southwest and can be found at most Latino markets. In this recipe I use Wondra flour, which is a great product that won't lump up, as a thickener for the sauce.

3 cups Low-Sodium Chicken Stock
   (see recipe on page 89)
2 cups macaroni
1 teaspoon taco seasoning mix, or Texas
   Jack's Seasoning (see recipe on page 89)
Dash granulated garlic
2 scallions, minced
1 stalk celery, minced
1/4 cup fresh parsley, minced
1/2 teaspoon balsamic vinegar
1 teaspoon dried epazote, optional
Salt and pepper, to taste
1 tablespoon Wondra flour

Bring the chicken stock to a boil and add the macaroni, taco seasoning, and garlic. Cook until the pasta is al dente. Drain the pasta, reserving the liquid in a sauce pan. Set pasta aside.

To the reserved liquid, add the scallions, celery, parsley, balsamic vinegar, epazote, salt, and pepper. Bring the sauce back to a simmer, and add the Wondra Flour. Continue to simmer, stirring constantly, until the sauce thickens. Pour over the macaroni and serve.

Makes 4-6 Servings

nutritional facts
per serving

Calories 149
Total Fat 2g
Cholesterol 0mg
Sodium 41mg
Total Carbohydrate 29g
Dietary Fiber 1g
Protein 10g

not just another coleslaw

This is my favorite rainy day coleslaw. Make a big batch and keep it handy to serve as a side dish at lunch or as a tasty snack for your midday meal.

 1 medium head of cabbage, chopped
 1 medium white onion, minced
 1 tablespoon chopped sun-dried tomatoes
 1 cup chopped green bell pepper
 1 clove garlic, minced
 1/2 cup sultana raisins
 1 tablespoon imitation bacon bits
 1 tablespoon pickle relish
 1 cup low-fat mayonnaise
 1/4 cup low-fat evaporated milk
 1/4 cup German mustard
 1/2 teaspoon Splenda sugar substitute
 1/4 teaspoon salt substitute

Combine all ingredients in a deep bowl and mix thoroughly. Refrigerate for at least 1 hour to allow the flavors to blend. Serve as a side dish or as a light and tasty meal.

Makes 12 Servings

nutritional facts
per serving

Calories 110
Total Fat 6g
Cholesterol 7mg
Sodium 209mg
Total Carbohydrate 14g
Dietary Fiber 3g
Protein 2g

pasta, turkey, and cheese salad

During the holiday season, everyone has leftover turkey. This recipe will help you use up some of that delicious meat.

3 cups cooked macaroni

1/2 cup cooked and diced turkey breast

1/3 pound cubed Cheddar cheese

1/4 cup minced white onion

2 tablespoons minced red bell pepper

2 tablespoons minced green bell pepper

1 cup low-fat mayonnaise

1/4 teaspoon minced fresh dill

1/4 teaspoon garlic powder

1/4 teaspoon celery seeds

1/4 teaspoon Old Bay Seasoning

Dash salt substitute

Dash black pepper

Fresh basil

Combine the cooked macaroni, turkey, cheese, onion, red bell pepper, green bell pepper, and mayonnaise. Stir to coat well. In a mortar add all spices, except the fresh basil, and crush to release the flavors. Add the spices to the salad and fold. Refrigerate for at least 1 hour to allow the flavors to blend. Garnish with fresh basil before serving.

Makes 6-8 Servings

nutritional facts
per serving

Calories 312
Total Fat 13*g*
Cholesterol 34*mg*
Sodium 295*mg*
Total Carbohydrate 35*g*
Dietary Fiber 1*g*
Protein 12*g*

pedro's pasta salad

Raviolini, those miniature, packaged raviolis you see at your favorite Italian deli, are the perfect size for salads. I use the multi-colored variety when I prepare this recipe.

1 cup cheese-filled raviolini
1/4 cup chopped fresh parsley
1/2 cup low-fat mayonnaise
1 tablespoon Parmesan cheese
1/2 cup cubed Feta cheese
1 tablespoon capers
1/4 cup chopped red bell pepper
1 scallion, minced
1/4 teaspoon paprika
1/4 teaspoon salt substitute, or to taste

Prepare the raviolini as directed on the package. Drain and rinse with cold water. Combine the pasta with all remaining ingredients, and mix thoroughly. Refrigerate for 1 hour before serving.

Makes 6-8 Servings

nutritional facts
per serving

Calories 111
Total Fat 7g
Cholesterol 40mg
Sodium 321mg
Total Carbohydrate 8g
Dietary Fiber trace
Protein 4g

rainbow pasta salad

This is a very colorful salad, and the flavors of the fennel and ginger make this dish stand on its own. For even more flavor add minced radishes and capers.

1 tablespoon fennel seed

1 teaspoon taco seasoning

1/2 teaspoon celery seeds

1 teaspoon garlic powder

1/2 teaspoon onion powder

1/4 teaspoon salt substitute

1/4 teaspoon white pepper

1/2 teaspoon turmeric

2 cups small shell macaroni, cooked al dente

2 cups rotini, cooked al dente

6 tablespoons extra virgin olive oil

1 small slice ginger root, minced

3 shallots, minced

1 stalk celery, diced

1/2 red bell pepper, minced

8 black olives, pitted and chopped

2 tablespoons balsamic vinegar

6 ounces mushroom caps

1/2 cup green taco sauce

Combine the fennel seeds, taco seasoning, celery seeds, garlic powder, onion powder, salt substitute, white pepper, and turmeric in a mortar. Crush the spices to release the flavors. Combine with the remaining ingredients in a large bowl, and mix well. Refrigerate for 1 hour to blend flavors. Serve chilled.

Makes 6-8 Servings

nutritional facts
Per Serving

Calories 238
Total Fat 11g
Cholesterol *trace*
Sodium 118mg
Total Carbohydrate 30g
Dietary Fiber 2g
Protein 5g

sunday brunch potato salad

My wife, Jodi, loves potatoes. Mashed, fried, baked—no matter how you prepare a spud, she'll savor it. The use of dark chili powder and a few drops of hot sauce give this salad just the right southwestern touch.

5 red potatoes, peeled and cut into
   1/2-inch cubes
3/4 cup egg substitute, hard-cooked
   and chopped
2 scallions, chopped
1/2 cup chopped red bell pepper
2 mushroom caps, chopped
1 tablespoon German mustard
1/2 cup low-fat mayonnaise
1/4 teaspoon crushed celery seeds
1/4 teaspoon garlic powder
1/4 teaspoon dark chili powder
1/4 teaspoon salt substitute
1/4 teaspoon white pepper
1/4 cup chopped fresh parsley
Dash of Tabasco Chipotle Pepper Sauce,
   or your favorite hot sauce

In a stew pot, add the potatoes and enough water to cover; bring to a boil and cook until the potatoes can be easily pierced with a toothpick. Drain the potatoes. Combine all ingredients in a deep bowl and gently stir to mix. Refrigerate for 1 hour or overnight. Serve chilled.

Makes 6-8 Servings

nutritional facts
Per Serving

Calories 128
Total Fat 5g
Cholesterol 74mg
Sodium 127mg
Total Carbohydrate 18g
Dietary Fiber 2g
Protein 4g

main meals

buttermilk meatloaf

I serve this tasty meatloaf covered with Spicy Tomato Sauce (see recipe on page 94). If you have leftovers, create a meatloaf sandwich topped with hot mustard and home-grown tomatoes.

1/2 teaspoon caraway seeds
1/4 teaspoon tarragon
1/4 teaspoon celery seeds
1/4 teaspoon sage
1/4 teaspoon black pepper
1/4 teaspoon salt substitute
1 cup low-fat buttermilk
2 pounds ground beef
1/4 cup egg substitute
1 cup diced white onion
1 cup diced green chiles
1 cup diced celery
1 cup bread crumbs
Spicy Tomato Sauce, optional

Combine the caraway seeds, tarragon, celery seeds, sage, pepper, and salt substitute in a mortar and grind to release flavors. Add spice mix to buttermilk and let set for 15 minutes.

Preheat the oven to 350° F. In a deep bowl, add the ground sirloin, egg substitute, onion, green chiles, celery, bread crumbs, and buttermilk mix. Mix until all the buttermilk is absorbed into the meat. Put the meatloaf mix in an 8 x 8-inch casserole dish and cover with aluminum foil. Bake for 1 1/2 hours. Remove from the oven to cool. If desired, add a spoonful of Spicy Tomato Sauce over the top before serving.

Makes 8 Servings

nutritional facts
per serving

Calories 362
Total Fat 21g
Cholesterol 80mg
Sodium 253mg
Total Carbohydrate 16g
Dietary Fiber 1g
Protein 26g

supreme meatballs and fettuccine

This recipe is tasty and easy to prepare. Just put the meatballs, sauce, and wine into the slow cooker and let it do its thing. Serve it over a warm plate of fettuccine with a fresh garden salad on the side.

    8 Spiced Veal Meatballs (see recipe on
        page 52)
    1 cup Plata Sonora Sauce (see recipe on
        page 93)
    1 cup dry white wine
    1/2 pound cooked fettuccine

Place the meatballs, sauce, and wine in your slow cooker. Cover and cook on low for 4 to 6 hours. The sauce will thicken as it cooks. Before serving, add the cooked fettuccine to the slow cooker and cook for 2 to 3 minutes more to warm the pasta. Serve immediately.

Makes 4 Servings

nutritional facts
per serving

Calories 487
Total Fat 12g
Cholesterol 54mg
Sodium 528mg
Total Carbohydrate 53g
Dietary Fiber 2g
Protein 27g

concho corned beef

I serve this Southwest corned beef specialty at my St. Patrick's Day parties. Just add some boiled new potatoes, chopped carrots, and green chiles on the side, and you'll be the hit of the party.

    2 cups water
    3 cans light beer, at room temperature
    1 teaspoon pickling spice
    4 tablespoons green taco sauce
    4 pounds corned beef brisket
    1 small white onion, chopped
    1/2 cup chopped red bell peppers
    1/2 cup chopped green bell peppers
    1/4 teaspoon Cajun seasoning

Combine all ingredients in a slow cooker. Cover and cook on low for 6 to 8 hours. Serve warm with fresh tortillas.

Makes 4-6 Servings

nutritional facts
per serving

Calories 329
Total Fat 22g
Cholesterol 81mg
Sodium 215mg
Total Carbohydrate 3g
Dietary Fiber *trace*
Protein 22g

machaca

Machaca is used in many southwestern recipes, including Ropa con Arroz (see recipe on page 48), and as a stuffing for enchiladas, tamales, burritos, and tacos. It's also used in Caribbean and South American dishes and is often called shredded or pulled beef.

- 4 pounds beef brisket, fat trimmed off
- 4 cloves garlic, minced
- 1 bay leaf
- 1 large white onion, sliced 1/2-inch thick
- 4 ounces tomato sauce, El Pato preferred
- 2 tablespoons chili powder
- 1/2 teaspoon salt substitute
- 1/2 teaspoon white pepper
- 8 cups water

Combine all ingredients in a deep stew pot. Bring to a boil, and then reduce to a simmer. Cover and let cook for 3 to 4 hours, making sure to add more water in 1/2 cup increments to keep the meat covered.

Remove the brisket and drain off the liquid. Shred the beef with a fork and serve immediately in tacos, burritos, tamales, or your favorite Mexican dish.

Makes 16 Servings

nutritional facts
per serving

Calories 338
Total Fat 27g
Cholesterol 79mg
Sodium 127mg
Total Carbohydrate 2g
Dietary Fiber 1g
Protein 21g

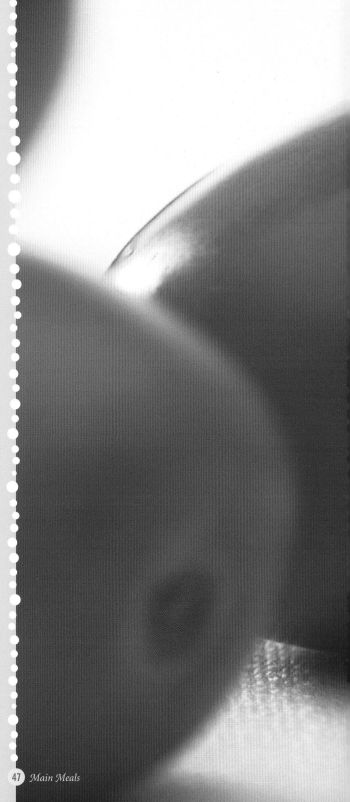

ropa con arroz

Now here's a great recipe for a family gathering that is perfect for the kids. You might say that Ropa, or pulled beef, is the Southwest's answer to Sloppy Joes. I like filling corn or flour tortillas with this beef and rice mixture for a great Mexican-style meal.

1 tablespoon canola oil
1 pound Machaca (see recipe on page 47)
1 medium red bell pepper, sliced
2 tomatoes, chopped
1 small white onion, thinly sliced
1/2 teaspoon ground cumin
1/2 teaspoon salt substitute
1 jalapeño chile, minced
1 cup beer, Negra Modelo preferred
2 cups cooked rice, warmed
1 cup chopped jicama
1/4 cup minced fresh cilantro

Heat a skillet until a drop of water quickly sizzles away. Add the canola oil and stir to coat the skillet. Add the machaca, bell pepper, tomatoes, onion, cumin, salt substitute, jalapeño, and beer. Bring to a boil, reduce to a simmer, and let cook for 15 minutes. Serve over equal portions of rice. Garnish each plate with jicama and cilantro.

Makes 4-6 Servings

nutritional facts
per serving

Calories 373
Total Fat 21g
Cholesterol 53mg
Sodium 96mg
Total Carbohydrate 27g
Dietary Fiber 3g
Protein 17g

grilled chipotle honey mustard t-bone steaks

If you like honey mustard dressing, then you will enjoy the zesty flavor of these grilled steaks. I make extra sauce for use on grilled chicken and pork chops.

4 T-bone steaks, fat trimmed off
1 chipotle chile in adobo sauce, finely minced
2 tablespoons brown mustard, or other dark mustard
1 tablespoon minced fresh cilantro
1 tablespoon honey
1 tablespoon balsamic vinegar
1/2 cup white wine
1/4 teaspoon ground black pepper

Bring the steaks to room temperature. In a deep mixing bowl, combine the chipotle chile, mustard, cilantro, honey, balsamic vinegar, wine, and black pepper. Mix well. Dredge the steaks in the chipotle honey mustard sauce and set aside.

Grill the steaks over a hot grill for 10 to 15 minutes per side depending on desired doneness. Serve immediately with a little of the extra sauce drizzled over the top.

Makes 4 Servings

nutritional facts
per serving

Calories 197
Total Fat 8g
Cholesterol 55mg
Sodium 184mg
Total Carbohydrate 6g
Dietary Fiber *trace*
Protein 21g

grilled jalapeño burgers

Ready for a zesty, low-carbohydrate hamburger? Then try this recipe for a flavorful grilled treat. This burger goes perfectly with my April on the Patio Potato Salad (see recipe on page 31). You can serve these burgers with or without a bun, or add a slab of low-fat cheese for a tasty Southwest cheeseburger.

1 pound ground beef
1/2 cup minced onion
1 jalapeño chile, finely minced
2 tablespoons egg substitute, optional
1 tablespoon low-fat evaporated milk
Freshly ground black pepper
1/4 teaspoon salt substitute
Low-carb hamburger buns, optional

Combine the ground beef, onion, jalapeño, egg substitute, evaporated milk, pepper, and salt substitute. Mix thoroughly. Form into 4 individual patties.

Grill the hamburgers over moderate heat for 5 minutes. Turn over the hamburgers and grill until done to your liking. Serve on a lightly toasted bun, if desired, with your favorite fixings.

Makes 4 Servings

nutritional facts
per serving

Calories 289
Total Fat 20*g*
Cholesterol 79*mg*
Sodium 95*mg*
Total Carbohydrate 3*g*
Dietary Fiber *trace*
Protein 23*g*

spiced veal meatballs

Look no further for the most delicious southwestern meat-balls. They are perfect when served over a hot bowl of noodles or as the main ingredient in El Paso Albóndigas Soup (see recipe on page 27). They are very easy to make and will freeze for later use.

1 pound ground veal
1/4 cup minced scallions
1/4 cup bread crumbs
1/4 cup egg substitute
1/8 teaspoon nutmeg
1/8 teaspoon ground ginger
1 teaspoon hot sauce
1 tablespoon canola oil
1/2 cup water

Combine all ingredients, except for the canola oil and water, in a deep bowl and mix thoroughly. Roll into 1-inch balls. You should have about 14 to 16 meatballs.

Heat a deep skillet until a drop of water quickly sizzles away. Add the canola oil to coat the bottom of the skillet. Cook the meatballs, turning often until browned. Add the water, cover, and simmer for 15 to 20 minutes. Serve immediately or refrigerate for later use.

Makes 4-6 Servings

nutritional facts
per serving

Calories 184
Total Fat 9g
Cholesterol 62mg
Sodium 169mg
Total Carbohydrate 7g
Dietary Fiber trace
Protein 17g

mojave sausage

Mojave Sausage is a staple in my kitchen. I use it to make my award-winning Chile Verde (see recipe on page 25) and as a filler in dishes such as cheese and sausage rellenos. It's also a great breakfast sausage.

1 pound ground pork shoulder
1 teaspoon ground cumin
1/2 teaspoon garlic powder
1/2 teaspoon chili powder
1/4 teaspoon fresh sage
Dash salt substitute

Mix all ingredients together in a medium bowl. Cover and refrigerate for at least 1 hour to allow the flavors to blend.

Heat a large skillet until a drop of water quickly sizzles away. Add the sausage mix, and brown until cooked through. Drain, and use in your favorite recipes.

Makes about 4 Servings

nutritional facts
per serving

Calories 205
Total Fat 15g
Cholesterol 60mg
Sodium 59mg
Total Carbohydrate 1g
Dietary Fiber *trace*
Protein 15g

pork tamale meat

This easy-to-make recipe is a great filling for tamales and broiled Portobello mushrooms. You can also reserve the broth and use it as a base for making Pablito's Black Beans (see recipe on page 80).

4 pounds pork shoulder roast, on the bone
2 cloves garlic, cut in half
1 teaspoon salt substitute
1 small onion, minced
1/2 cup chopped red bell pepper
8 cups water
2 cups Low-Sodium Chicken Stock
   (see recipe on page 89)
4 ounces tomato sauce, El Pato preferred
1/2 teaspoon ground cumin
1/2 teaspoon cardamom
1/4 teaspoon hot red chili powder
1 bay leaf

Combine all ingredients in a stew pot or Dutch oven. Bring to a boil and let cook for 30 minutes. Reduce to the lowest heat, cover, and let cook for 2 hours. Remove the meat and let it cool. With a fork, shred the pork meat.

Add the shredded pork to Portobello mushroom caps, or use in stews, enchiladas, tamales, or other favorite Southwest recipes. Refrigerate the unused portion in an air-tight container for up to 1 week.

Makes 24 Servings

nutritional facts
per serving

Calories 140
Total Fat 10g
Cholesterol 40mg
Sodium 112mg
Total Carbohydrate 1g
Dietary Fiber *trace*
Protein 11g

fettuccine and ham with orange cream sauce

This is a rich and tasty recipe with a delicate hint of orange flavor. Balance it with a light salad and your favorite vinaigrette dressing.

4 quarts cold water, lightly salted

1/2 pound fettuccine

1 teaspoon Tabasco

2 tablespoons extra virgin olive oil

1 teaspoon salt substitute

1/2 teaspoon white pepper

1/8 teaspoon nutmeg

1/8 teaspoon dried oregano, the Mexican variety preferred

1/8 teaspoon tarragon

1/4 pound cubed ham

1/4 cup minced white onion

1/4 cup minced green bell pepper

1 small garlic clove, finely minced

1/2 cup Mock Sour Cream (see recipe on page 97)

1/2 cup low-fat cottage cheese

1/2 cup cubed Queso Fresco

1/2 cup orange juice

1/2 cup minced red bell pepper

4 sprigs fresh cilantro

Bring the water to a brisk boil and cook the fettuccine until it is al dente. Drain the pasta and run cold water over it to stop the cooking process. Place the pasta in a deep bowl, add the Tabasco and one tablespoon of the olive oil, and mix to coat. Set aside.

In a mortar, combine the salt substitute, pepper, and nutmeg. Crush to a fine powder. Add the oregano and tarragon, and stir to blend. Mix the spices in with the pasta. Set aside.

Heat a large skillet until a drop of water quickly sizzles away. Add the remaining olive oil, the ham, onion, bell pepper, and garlic. Sauté until the onion is limp. Reduce the heat to low. Add the Mock Sour Cream and cottage cheese. Stir until the mixture starts to steam or gently bubble. Add the cubed Queso Fresco and stir constantly until the cubes are dissolved. Add the orange juice and bring back to a simmer. Cover for 10 minutes, stirring every 1 to 2 minutes.

Combine the seasoned pasta with the sauce and cook for 1 minute, or until the pasta is heated through. Garnish with the red bell pepper and cilantro, and serve immediately.

Makes 6-8 Servings

nutritional facts
per serving

Calories 242
Total Fat 7g
Cholesterol 14mg
Sodium 518mg
Total Carbohydrate 28g
Dietary Fiber 1g
Protein 17g

flavor border barbecued ham

Why do I use the term Flavor Border? I use this term to define the powerful mixture of Mexican flavors with our American ingredients, thereby creating the wonderful cuisine of the Southwest. Try this recipe out on your grill, and it'll soon be one of your favorites, too.

1 (10-pound) smoked ham
2 cups water
1/2 cup Splenda sugar substitute
1 teaspoon salt substitute
1/2 cup green taco sauce
1 medium orange, thinly sliced

Remove the ham from its package and reserve the liquid. Cut the skin of the ham, about 1/2-inch deep, vertically from top to bottom in several places, about 6 to 8 cuts in all. Make additional 1/2-inch horizontal cuts through the skin, 5 to 6 cuts to form diamond-shaped cubes. Remove the top row of cubes from the ham and set aside. Place the ham, butt side down, in an ovenproof container. Add the reserved liquid and the water. Insert a meat thermometer in the thickest part of the ham.

Combine the Splenda and salt substitute and spread around the top section of the ham where the ham cubes were removed. Spoon the taco sauce over the salt mix. With wooden tooth picks, secure the orange slices to the upper side of the ham. Return the extra cubed ham slices to the pan.

Preheat the grill to 200° F. Place the ham container in the middle of the grill, and close the cover. Try to maintain a minimum of 200° F. and a maximum of 225° F. by regulating the vents on the grill. Baste every 15 minutes with the liquid in the bottom of the pan. Add extra water, if needed, one cup at a time to avoid boiling away the basting liquid. Bake until the meat thermometer reads 145° F. Remove from the grill and transfer to a platter. Drizzle the sauce from the pan over the ham, and serve warm.

Makes 12-14 Servings

nutritional facts
per serving

Calories 18
Total Fat 1*g*
Cholesterol 4*mg*
Sodium 138*mg*
Total Carbohydrate 20*g*
Dietary Fiber *trace*
Protein 1*g*

sweet southwest-style pork chops

My recipe partially cooks the chops on the stovetop and then takes them to the oven where they are baked covered with rich fruit. I suggest you reserve the baking juices and, adding a little white wine and flour (or Wondra flour), make gravy to ladle over the ribs. Serve with a side of Bronco Beans (see recipe on page 74) or a crisp Romaine salad.

8 large boneless pork chops, cut 1-inch thick
2 teaspoons crushed celery seeds
1 tablespoon cracked black pepper
3 tablespoons olive oil
1 clove garlic, finely minced
1/4 cup brandy
1/2 cup tomato juice, spicy preferred
1 mango, chopped
1 small papaya, chopped
1 cup pineapple chunks in juice

Preheat the oven to 375° F. Coat the chops with celery seeds and black pepper. Heat a skillet until a drop of water quickly sizzles away. Add the olive oil and stir to coat the pan. Braise the chops until they are lightly brown on all sides. Remove the chops to a plate, add the garlic to the pan, and deglaze the pan with the brandy.

Pour the deglazed sauce into a 10 x 13-inch casserole dish and spread to coat the bottom of the dish. Pour the tomato juice into the casserole dish, and then add the browned chops, separating them so they don't touch. Top the chops with the mango, papaya, pineapple chunks, and pineapple juice. Cover the casserole dish with aluminum foil and bake for 2 hours. Remove from the oven, place the chops on individual serving plates, top with some of the fruit and sauce, and serve warm.

Makes 6-8 Servings

nutritional facts
per serving

Calories 665
Total Fat 39g
Cholesterol 121mg
Sodium 202mg
Total Carbohydrate 29g
Dietary Fiber 4g
Protein 42g

little birds

These spicy stuffed chicken rolls are fun and easy to make. For a zestier flavor add a minced chipotle chile to the stuffing mix. I like to serve these delicious birds on a thick bed of vermicelli noodles.

4 boneless, skinless chicken breasts
1 teaspoon salsa seasoning
4 ounces lean ground beef, cooked
2 tablespoons Neufchatel cheese
2 tablespoons Shedd's Spread
  Country Crock
2 large mushroom caps, minced
1 large shallot, minced
1 teaspoon Creole seasoning
All-purpose flour
2 tablespoons canola oil
1/2 cup light beer
1/2 cup green enchilada sauce
1/4 cup Mock Sour Cream
  (see recipe on page 97)

Pound the chicken breasts until they are very thin, about 1/4-inch. Coat with the salsa seasoning and refrigerate for at least 1 hour.

In a medium bowl, combine the lean ground beef, Neufchatel cheese, Shedd's Spread, mushrooms, shallot, and Creole seasoning. Mix thoroughly. Form into a roll, cover with plastic wrap, and refrigerate for 30 minutes.

Remove the stuffing roll from the refrigerator. Form into 4 equal-sized rolls. Add some flour to a mixing bowl. Remove the chicken from the refrigerator and place on a cutting board.

Place a stuffing roll on top of each breast, and starting from the wide edge of the breast, roll the chicken breast once around the roll, making sure to leave a little of the chicken unrolled. Fold in the edges of the chicken and finish the roll to the end. Seal tightly with a toothpick. Dredge the stuffed bird in the flour and set aside. Repeat the process until all the Little Birds are done, adding more flour as needed.

Preheat the oven to its lowest setting, about 150° F. Heat a large skillet until a drop of water quickly sizzles away. Add the canola oil and swirl to coat the bottom of the skillet. Fry the Little Birds in batches of two until browned on all sides. Remove to a platter and keep warm in the oven. Repeat this procedure for the remaining birds.

Pour off the excess oil, and return the skillet to the stove. Add the light beer and green enchilada sauce to the skillet. Bring to a simmer, scraping the skillet to loosen the remaining drippings. Continue cooking to thicken the sauce, about 5 minutes. Remove the Little Birds to individual plates, and serve topped with the beer sauce and a dab of Mock Sour Cream.

Makes 4 Servings

nutritional facts
per serving

Calories 372
Total Fat 22g
Cholesterol 121mg
Sodium 225mg
Total Carbohydrate 4g
Dietary Fiber 1g
Protein 37g

grilled chicken fajitas

Chicken fajitas are great off the grill. They are simple to make and tasty to eat. Add a spicy cup of Chile Verde (see recipe on page 25) and you'll have a complete meal.

2 boneless, skinless chicken breasts
1 tablespoon canola oil
1 teaspoon fresh lemon juice
2 tablespoons dry white wine
1 clove garlic, finely minced
1 teaspoon Tabasco
1/2 teaspoon dried oregano, the Mexican
    variety preferred
1/4 teaspoon salt substitute
1 small red onion, sliced 1/4-inch thick
1 green bell pepper, sliced 1/4-inch thick
6 (6-inch) low-carbohydrate flour tortillas
1 small tomato, chopped
3 green chiles, roasted, peeled, and
    sliced 1/4-inch thick

With the flat side of a meat cleaver or heavy object such as a rolling pin, flatten the chicken breasts to 1/4-inch. Cut the breasts in 1/2-inch strips, and set aside. In a medium bowl, combine the canola oil, lemon juice, dry white wine, garlic, Tabasco, oregano, and salt substitute. Add the chicken breast strips to the marinade and stir to coat. Cover and refrigerate for at least 1 hour.

Heat a grill to moderate heat, about 250° F. While the grill is heating up, remove the chicken and marinade from the refrigerator and bring to room temperature. Grill the chicken strips, red onion, and bell pepper, turning once.

Warm the tortillas by placing them in a damp towel and heating them in a microwave for 15 seconds or steaming them in a frying pan over low heat. Add equal amounts of grilled chicken strips, grilled vegetables, chopped tomato, and green chile slices to each fajita and serve. Add your favorite sauce as a seasoning, if desired.

Makes 6 Servings

nutritional facts
per serving

Calories 146
Total Fat 5g
Cholesterol 23mg
Sodium 641mg
Total Carbohydrates 18g
Dietary Fiber 3g
Protein 15g

red pepper chicken breasts

Here's a simple and tasty chicken breast entrée. I like to serve the breasts with Dilled Parmesan Sauce (see recipe on page 91).

- 3 tablespoons extra virgin olive oil
- 4 boneless, skinless chicken breasts
- 2 tablespoons salt-free Cajun seasoning
- 1 teaspoon garlic powder
- 4 thin slices red bell pepper
- 4 tablespoons shredded Romano cheese
- 1 (4-ounce) can diced green chiles, optional

Preheat the oven to 375° F. Spread one tablespoon of the olive oil in a 13 x 9-inch casserole dish, and swirl to coat the bottom. Add the chicken breasts and coat with the remaining oil. Sprinkle the Cajun seasoning and garlic powder on the chicken breasts. Roll the breasts over and coat with seasoning. Place equal amounts of bell pepper slices on each breast. Add the Romano cheese. Cover the casserole dish with aluminum foil and bake for 2 hours. Remove the chicken and bell peppers to individual plates, garnish with diced green chiles, if desired, and serve immediately.

Makes 4 Servings

nutritional facts
per serving

Calories 400
Total Fat 26*g*
Cholesterol 100*mg*
Sodium 178*mg*
Total Carbohydrate 8*g*
Dietary Fiber 2*g*
Protein 34*g*

chicken breast la jolla

This is the chicken used in La Jolla Fiesta Chicken (see recipe on page 63). Whether you use this tasty chicken breast with other recipes or as a stand alone meal, you'll be delighted with its outstanding flavor.

1 teaspoon granulated garlic
1 teaspoon paprika
1 teaspoon minced ginger
1/2 teaspoon ground cumin
1/4 teaspoon white pepper
1/4 cup pineapple juice
1/4 cup low-sodium soy sauce
8 boneless, skinless chicken breasts

Combine the garlic, paprika, ginger, cumin, pepper, and pineapple juice. Blend thoroughly. Pour over the chicken breasts and marinate for at least 1 hour.

Grill the breasts for about 10 minutes per side. Baste with the marinade while grilling. Serve over a bed of rice or in La Jolla Fiesta Chicken.

Makes 4 Servings

nutritional facts
per serving

Calories 142
Total Fat 2g
Cholesterol 68mg
Sodium 377mg
Total Carbohydrate 3g
Dietary Fiber *trace*
Protein 28g

la jolla fiesta chicken

La Jolla is one of the premier small cities in California, and it is gifted with many southwestern restaurants. This delicious grilled chicken is similar to a dish I had at a small restaurant along the Camino de Real several years ago. Serve this chicken with a Caesar's Salad and a nice white wine.

- 4 servings of Chicken Breast La Jolla (see recipe on page 61)
- 4 pineapple rings in juice
- 4 thin slices red onion
- 2 tablespoons Parmesan El Rico (see recipe on page 97)
- 4 small mushroom caps, halved
- 4 thin slices green bell pepper
- 4 thin slices crookneck squash
- 4 thin slices red bell pepper
- 4 teaspoons Shedd's Spread Country Crock
- 4 tablespoons orange juice

Separate a 12-inch square piece of heavy aluminum foil into 4 equal pieces, about 4 x 3-inches each. Make 4 deep pockets big enough to hold the chicken. To each pouch add 1 chicken breast, 1 pineapple ring, 1 slice of red onion, 1 tablespoon of Parmesan El Rico, 1 chopped mushroom cap, 1 slice of green bell pepper, 1 slice of squash, 1 slice of red bell pepper, 1 teaspoon of Shedd's Spread, and 1 tablespoon of orange juice. Seal the pouches to form 4 tents.

Place each pouch on a hot grill and cook for 5 to 10 minutes, or until steam rises from inside the packets. Carefully remove the layers from the packet, place decoratively on plates, and serve immediately.

Makes 4 Servings

nutritional facts
per serving

Calories 126
Total Fat 3g
Cholesterol 15mg
Sodium 159mg
Total Carbohydrate 21g
Dietary Fiber 3g
Protein 6g

chile and crab quiche

Crab claw meat is very versatile, and I often serve this simple-to-make quiche for breakfast or brunch. Some thickly sliced ham and champagne mimosas add a nice touch.

6 ounces crab claw meat
1 1/2 cups shredded Cheddar cheese
1/2 cup chopped green chiles
1/4 cup chopped scallions
1 1/2 cups egg substitute
12 ounces low-fat evaporated milk
3/4 teaspoon Colman's English Mustard
1/2 teaspoon salt substitute
1/4 teaspoon nutmeg
Dash paprika
Dash hot sauce

Preheat the oven to 400° F. In a deep bowl, combine the crab, cheese, chiles, and scallions, and mix thoroughly. Spray a deep pie pan or quiche dish with vegetable cooking spray. Add the crab mix and form tightly against the sides and bottom to form a crust.

In another bowl, combine the egg substitute, evaporated milk, mustard, salt substitute, nutmeg, paprika, and hot sauce. Mix thoroughly. Slowly pour the mix over the crab crust. Bake, uncovered, for 25 to 30 minutes, or until a tooth-pick or butter knife inserted in the middle comes out clean. Let cool for 10 minutes. Cut into quarters and serve warm.

Makes 4-6 Servings

nutritional facts
per serving

Calories 167
Total Fat 7g
Cholesterol 16mg
Sodium 447mg
Total Carbohydrate 8g
Dietary Fiber *trace*
Protein 18g

steamed clams in cilantro and wine sauce

This is a Spanish Basque-style recipe similar to one I had while fishing off the east coast of Baja California. You can use any of your favorite clams or mussels with this recipe. Serve this dish with a large loaf of sourdough bread to sop up the juices. A cold Mexican beer is a must with these delicious clams.

24 cherrystone clams, or your
   favorite variety
2 teaspoons cornmeal
1 tablespoon extra virgin olive oil
1/4 cup minced scallions
1 clove garlic, minced
1/2 cup chopped fresh cilantro
1 cup dry white wine
2 tablespoons fresh lime juice
1/4 cup crushed tortilla chips
Limes wedges
Tabasco, optional

Place the clams in a large pan of cool water. Sprinkle the cornmeal over the water and let stand for 4 to 5 hours or over night. Rinse the clams in cold water, and then brush them with a stiff brush to remove any excess sand and particles.

Heat a Dutch oven or deep skillet until a drop of water quickly sizzles away. Add the olive oil and swirl to coat. Add the scallions and garlic. Sauté for 2 minutes. Add the clams, cilantro, wine, and lime juice. Cover and steam until the clams open (times vary, so just be patient). Add the crushed tortilla chips, and cover for 1 more minute. Divide the clams into equal portions, place in serving bowls, and spoon the sauce over the top. Serve at once.

Makes 4 Servings

nutritional facts
per serving

Calories 170
Total Fat 5g
Cholesterol 24mg
Sodium 110mg
Total Carbohydrate 12g
Dietary Fiber 1g
Protein 11g

teriyaki tuna steaks

Tuna and a barbecue grill complement each other, and this recipe is one of my favorites. To give it a Southwest touch, I serve this dish with Scallion-Cilantro Sauce (see recipe on page 92) and fresh lime wedges on the side.

1 tablespoon low-sodium teriyaki sauce

1 tablespoon fresh lime juice

1 clove garlic, minced

2 tablespoons olive oil

4 (1/4-pound) tuna steaks

Combine the teriyaki sauce, lime juice, garlic, and 1 table-spoon of the olive oil in a blender, and blend thoroughly. Pour over the tuna steaks and let marinate for 30 to 45 minutes.

Preheat the grill. Soak a clean cloth with the remaining tablespoon of olive oil, and coat the grates. Grill the steaks for 5 to 7 minutes, turning once. Brush the marinade over the steaks while grilling. Remove from the grill, place steaks on individual plates, and serve immediately.

Makes 4 Servings

nutritional facts
per serving

calories 203
total fat 9g
cholesterol 43mg
sodium 234mg
total carbohydrate 6g
dietary fiber *trace*
protein 27g

sea bass matamoras-style

I love sea bass. There's so much you can do with this fabulous white meat fish. The orange flavor of Cointreau adds a special touch to this method of preparation.

4 (1/4-pound) sea bass fillets
6 tablespoons canola oil
2 scallions, chopped
1/4 cup chopped fresh parsley
2 tablespoons fresh lemon juice
1 clove garlic, minced
1 teaspoon Cointreau, or any orange liqueur
1/4 teaspoon orange zest
1/2 teaspoon salt substitute
1/2 teaspoon white pepper
1/4 teaspoon crushed celery seeds
Lime wedges

Preheat the oven to 350° F. Dry the fillets with a paper towel or clean dish cloth. Place 3 tablespoons of the oil in the bottom of an 8 x 8-inch baking dish. Add half of the chopped scallions and half of the chopped parsley. Place the fillets in the baking dish on top of the scallions and parsley.

In a separate bowl, combine the lemon juice, the remaining 3 tablespoons of the canola oil, garlic, Cointreau, orange zest, salt substitute, pepper, and celery seeds. Mix well and spoon over the fillets. Sprinkle the remaining scallions and parsley over the top.

Cover the baking dish tightly with aluminum foil and bake for 20 to 25 minutes, or until the fish flakes easily. Remove from the oven and serve with freshly cut lime wedges on the side.

Makes 4 Servings

nutritional facts
Per Serving

Calories 326
Total Fat 23g
Cholesterol 53mg
Sodium 91mg
Total Carbohydrate 3g
Dietary Fiber *trace*
Protein 24g

cajun shrimp scampi

Louisiana is a hotbed of zesty Southwest flavors. Tabasco is made near New Orleans and the Cajun language is a mix of French, Spanish, English, and a smattering of Italian. This tasty recipe is a mix of all those diverse cultures.

3 tablespoons Shedd's Spread
   Country Crock
1 clove garlic, minced
1/4 cup minced red bell pepper
3 scallions, chopped
1 cup halved mushroom caps
1 pound shrimp, peeled and deveined
1 teaspoon Cajun seasoning, or
   taco seasoning
1/4 cup ricotta cheese
1/4 cup dark rum
1/4 cup Low-Sodium Chicken Stock
   (see recipe on page 89)
Tabasco, to taste
1/4 cup minced fresh basil
Lemon wedges

Heat a large skillet until a drop of water quickly sizzles away. Add the Shedd's Spread and swirl to coat. Add the garlic, bell pepper, scallions, and mushrooms, and sauté. Add the shrimp and cook until they are just starting to turn pink. Reduce to the lowest heat, and then sprinkle with Cajun seasoning and ricotta cheese. Swirl until the shrimp are totally pink, about 1 minute. Add the rum, and set aflame. Add the chicken stock and stir for a few minutes to mix the flavors. Add as many dashes of Tabasco as desired, and stir until well mixed. Remove from heat, add fresh basil, and serve immediately. Garnish with fresh lemon wedges on the side.

Makes 4-6 Servings

nutritional facts
per serving

Calories 290
Total Fat 8g
Cholesterol 166mg
Sodium 306mg
Total Carbohydrate 15g
Dietary Fiber 6g
Protein 36g

sunday morning crab and spinach crepes

It's Sunday morning and you have company coming over. Surprise everyone with these simple yet elegant crepes. This brunch is especially good when served with fresh mimosas.

1/4 cup spinach leaves, stems removed

1 tablespoon egg substitute

3 tablespoons Shedd's Spread Country Crock

1/2 teaspoon salsa seasoning, or Texas Jack's Seasoning (see recipe on page 89)

1/2 cup all-purpose flour

1 cup low-fat milk

1/2 pound chopped crab meat

6 thinly sliced mushrooms

1/2 cup Mock Sour Cream (see recipe on page 97)

1 clove garlic, finely minced

1/4 teaspoon paprika

1/4 cup shredded Cheddar cheese

Fresh cilantro

Preheat the oven to 375° F. To make the crepe batter, wash the spinach leaves and put into a food processor or blender. Add the egg substitute, 2 tablespoons of the Shedd's Spread, salsa seasoning, flour, and milk. Blend well for 30 seconds, and then pour into a bowl. Set aside.

In a separate bowl, add the crab, mushrooms, Mock Sour Cream, garlic, and paprika. Mix thoroughly. Set the filling aside.

Heat a 7-inch sauté pan with smooth sides over medium heat until a drop of water quickly sizzles away. Add the remaining 1 tablespoon of Shedd's Spread to the hot pan, add a tablespoon of the batter, and roll the pan to spread the batter evenly. Reduce the heat to low. Crepes will cook in approximately 30 seconds and should be almost paper thin. Don't turn. They will be done when they have lost their shine. The crepes should easily slide out of the pan. Handle the crepes carefully or they will pull apart. I slide them onto a salad platter that has been sprayed with vegetable or canola oil to let them cool. If the batter starts to thicken, you can thin it out with 1 or 2 teaspoons of water. Repeat this process until all crepes have been made.

Doing one crepe at a time, spread the crab mixture across one side of a crepe, and then roll into a tube. Continue until all remaining crepes have been filled. Place the rolled crepes in a 13 x 9-inch ovenproof dish. Sprinkle the shredded cheese over the crepes, and place the dish in the oven until cheese melts, about 4 to 5 minutes. Serve warm garnished with cilantro.

Makes 12 Servings

nutritional facts
per serving

Calories 118
Total Fat 5g
Cholesterol 30mg
Sodium 305mg
Total Carbohydrate 7g
Dietary Fiber trace
Protein 11g

vegetables

brown rice and red beans

This healthy recipe is my version of a Cajun favorite, and, as a bonus, it is full of dietary fiber and low on fat. Serve it on the side with your favorite Bayou entrée or my Concho Corned Beef (see recipe on page 46).

1 1/2 cups Low-Sodium Beef Stock
    (see recipe on page 87)
1 cup brown rice
2 tablespoons imitation bacon bits
1/2 cup chopped and sautéed green
    bell peppers
1 clove garlic, minced
2 scallions, chopped
1/2 teaspoon onion powder
1 bay leaf
2 cups cooked red beans
1 teaspoon Cajun seasoning
1/2 teaspoon chili powder

Combine all ingredients in a deep pot, and bring to a boil. Reduce to a low simmer, cover, and cook for 30 minutes. Serve warm with your favorite dish or alone with fresh tortillas.

Makes 6-8 Servings

nutritional facts
per serving

Calories 254
Total Fat 1g
Cholesterol 0mg
Sodium 178mg
Total Carbohydrate 48g
Dietary Fiber 12g
Protein 15g

bronco beans

Here's a side of real New Mexico cowboy beans. Try them with a hearty grilled sirloin steak or my tasty Sweet Southwest-Style Pork Chops (see recipe on page 57). There's not a cowboy around that doesn't savor a steaming pot of beans. Divvy up a bowl and talk cattle with the hands. Yee haw!

- 1 tablespoon canola oil
- 1 cup chopped white onions
- 1 cup chopped green bell pepper
- 2 cloves garlic, minced
- 1/4 cup imitation bacon bits
- 1 teaspoon salt substitute
- 2 cups Low-Sodium Chicken Stock (see recipe on page 89)
- 3 cups water
- 4 cups pinto beans, cleaned and washed
- 2 tablespoons dark molasses
- 2 tablespoons Texas Jack's Seasoning (see recipe on page 89)
- 1/4 teaspoon powdered jalapeño
- 1 bay leaf

Heat a deep pot or Dutch oven until a drop of water quickly sizzles away. Add the canola oil and stir to coat. Add the onion, bell pepper, and garlic, and lightly sauté. Add the remaining ingredients; bring to a boil and let cook for 15 minutes. Reduce to a bare simmer, cover, and let cook for 1 hour.

Remove from heat and let set for 30 minutes. Bring back to a boil, and then reduce again to a bare simmer. Add extra water, as needed, to barely cover the beans. Simmer for 2 hours more. When the beans are cooked through, remove from heat and serve immediately.

Makes about 4 Servings

nutritional facts
per serving

Calories 203
Total Fat 2g
Cholesterol *trace*
Sodium 117mg
Total Carbohydrate 35g
Dietary Fiber 13g
Protein 12g

buenos días papas

Serve these Good Morning Potatoes on the side with scrambled eggs and chorizo sausage. Add your favorite salsa for some spicy zest.

2 baking potatoes, quartered
1 medium white onion, chopped
1/2 head cabbage, chopped
1 poblano chile, chopped
2 tablespoons Shedd's Spread Country Crock
1/4 teaspoon Old Bay Seasoning
Dash salt substitute
1/4 cup low-fat evaporated milk

Combine all ingredients in a food processor and lightly chop. Heat a deep skillet until a drop of water quickly sizzles away. Cook the mixture until it starts to brown on the bottom. Turn and cook until brown on the other side. Serve immediately for breakfast, lunch, or dinner.

Makes 4-6 Servings

nutritional facts
per serving

Calories 124
Total Fat 2g
Cholesterol 1mg
Sodium 108mg
Total Carbohydrate 23g
Dietary Fiber 2g
Protein 4g

eggplant sonora with wild rice

To make this flavorful dish even spicier, use an authentic Mexican-style tomato sauce like El Pato. Serve as directed below, or, for variety, hard cook the egg substitute and serve on top as pictured.

1 large eggplant, sliced in 1/2-inch rounds
Salt substitute
2 cups fast-cooking long grain and
   wild rice
1 cup egg substitute
1/2 cup low-fat evaporated milk
2 tablespoons canola oil
1 cup diced tomatoes
1/2 cup diced green chiles
1 (8-ounce) can tomato sauce
1 cup Herdez Salsa Verde
1 cup bread crumbs
4 slices smoked Gouda cheese
1/2 cup shredded Cheddar cheese, or
   Mexican cheese mix

Preheat the oven to 350° F. In a large casserole dish, combine the prepared wild rice, diced tomatoes, green chiles, tomato sauce, and salsa. Mix to blend. Place a solid layer of eggplant slices over the rice mix. Combine the bread crumbs and both cheeses and cover the eggplant. Bake for 30 minutes. Serve warm.

Makes 4-6 Servings

nutritional facts
per serving

Calories 638
Total Fat 34g
Cholesterol 97mg
Sodium 261mg
Total Carbohydrate 45g
Dietary Fiber 3g
Protein 33g

Place the eggplant slices on a tray and sprinkle with salt substitute. Turn over and sprinkle the other side. Let sweat for 20 to 30 minutes.

In the meantime, prepare the rice as directed on the package, and set aside. In a deep bowl, combine the egg substitute and evaporated milk. Heat a skillet until a drop of water quickly sizzles away. Add the canola oil and spread to coat. Dry the eggplant with paper towels, dip each slice into the milk mixture to coat, and then brown on both sides. Set aside.

arroz a la sonora

This is my version of Spanish Rice, which is similar to the side dish served at many Mexican restaurants. The addition of chipotle, diced green chiles, and red onion gives it a Sonoran touch. I often serve this tasty and colorful dish with ham or chicken.

2 tablespoons canola oil

1 cup long grain white rice

1 tablespoon tomato paste

2 cloves garlic, minced

1 cup water

1 chipotle chile in adobo sauce,
   finely minced

1 (4-ounce) can diced green chiles

1 small red onion, chopped

1 serrano chile, finely minced

1 1/2 cups Low-Sodium Chicken Stock (see
   recipe on page 89)

1/2 teaspoon salt substitute, or to taste

1/2 cup diced carrots

1/2 cup frozen peas

Fresh cilantro

Heat a skillet until a drop of water quickly sizzles away. Add the oil and rice. Cook the rice just until it starts to brown. Strain the rice and return it to the skillet.

In a blender combine the tomato paste, garlic, and water, and purée. Pour the tomato mixture over the rice. Add all remaining ingredients, except for the cilantro. Bring to a slow boil and cook for 5 minutes, stirring often. Cover the skillet, reduce to low, and cook for 30 minutes, stirring every 10 minutes to avoid sticking.

Makes 4-6 Servings

nutritional facts
per serving

Calories 193
Total Fat 6g
Cholesterol *trace*
Sodium 68mg
Total Carbohydrates 32g
Dietary Fiber 2g
Protein 7g

francisco's potato hash browns

You won't find a better recipe for a brunch with your family and friends. The maple syrup flavor adds a special touch and separates this dish from the bland version offered at many restaurants. I often spoon a zesty salsa such as Roasted Green Tomato Salsa (see recipe on page 14) over the top.

3 large potatoes, sliced 1/4-inch thick
1 medium red onion, sliced 1/4-inch thick
1 cup water
2 tablespoons canola oil
1 small green bell pepper, diced
2 tablespoons maple syrup
1/4 teaspoon salt substitute
1/4 teaspoon black pepper
1 teaspoon salsa seasoning

Combine all ingredients in a deep skillet or Dutch oven. Bring to a boil. Cover and reduce to a simmer. Let cook for 30 minutes, stirring occasionally. Remove the cover and cook until the mix starts to brown on the bottom. Turn the potatoes and brown on the other side. Serve hot with your favorite salsa on top.

Makes 4-6 Servings

nutritional facts
per serving

Calories 173
Total Fat 7g
Cholesterol *trace*
Sodium 10mg
Total Carbohydrate 26g
Dietary Fiber 3g
Protein 3g

pablito's black beans

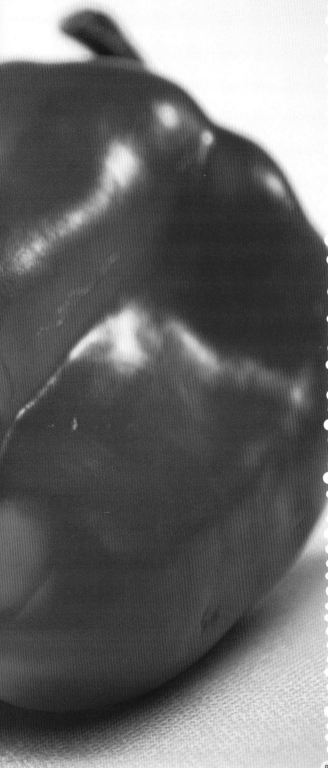

These tasty beans are great as a side dish or as an addition to soup. I also use Pablito's Black Beans on quesadillas, as fillers in cheese and black bean enchiladas, or as a stuffing for burritos or chimichangas.

1 pound black beans
4 cups water
1 bay leaf
2 cloves garlic, minced
1 medium yellow onion, chopped
1 stalk celery, minced
1 cup minced red bell pepper
2 tablespoons extra virgin olive oil
1 teaspoon salt substitute
Dash cayenne

Sort and wash the black beans. Add to a deep soup pot, cover with the water, and let soak for 1 hour. Add the remaining ingredients. Bring to a boil and let cook, covered, for 20 minutes. Remove the cover, reduce to a simmer, and let cook until the beans are soft, about 1 hour, stirring often to avoid sticking. Serve immediately with your favorite dish.

Makes 12 Servings

nutritional facts
per serving

Calories 156
Total Fat 3g
Cholesterol *trace*
Sodium 8mg
Total Carbohydrate 25g
Dietary Fiber 6g
Protein 8g

green tomatoes

This recipe was inspired when my garden produced an abundance of tomatoes. Unfortunately, they were all ripening at the same time, so I took advantage of the surplus crop and whipped up this tasty morsel. It makes a great side dish to accompany my Red Pepper Chicken Breasts (see recipe on page 60).

> 2 tablespoons extra virgin olive oil
> 1 tablespoon Shedd's Spread Country Crock
> 1/2 cup shredded Romano cheese
> 1/4 teaspoon chili powder
> 1/2 teaspoon Old Bay Seasoning
> 4 large green tomatoes, thickly sliced
> 3 tablespoons egg substitute
> Lemon slices

Preheat the oven to the lowest temperature, about 150° F. Heat a skillet until a drop of water quickly sizzles away. Add the olive oil and Shedd's Spread, and stir to coat the skillet.

In a bowl, combine the Romano cheese, chili powder, Old Bay Seasoning, and mix thoroughly. Set aside. To another bowl, add the egg substitute. Dredge several tomato slices in the egg substitute, and then coat both sides in the Romano cheese mixture. Fry the slices until brown on both sides, drain on a paper towel, and keep warm in the oven. Continue until all tomatoes are fried. Serve with lemon slices on the side.

Makes 8 Servings

nutritional facts
per serving

Calories 93
Total Fat 7g
Cholesterol 7mg
Sodium 158mg
Total Carbohydrate 5g
Dietary Fiber 1g
Protein 4g

cajun-style grilled sweet onions

This is a tasty grilled side dish that will enhance your afternoon barbecue party. I often serve these sweet and spicy onions with grilled andouille sausage or on grilled hamburgers.

1 tablespoon extra virgin olive oil
1 teaspoon honey
1/2 teaspoon Cajun seasoning
1/2 teaspoon balsamic vinegar
1/4 teaspoon salt substitute
1 large red onion, thinly sliced

In a mixing bowl combine the olive oil, honey, Cajun seasoning, vinegar, and salt substitute. Mix thoroughly. Add the onion and mix to coat.

Make a pouch by wrapping aluminum foil around a 12-ounce tuna can (or similar) to form a pocket about 6-inches deep. Make a pouch for each of the 4 servings. Add equal amounts of the onions to each pouch. Drizzle remaining oil; mix equally into each pouch. Seal the pouches. Grill for 15 to 20 minutes on the top shelf or edge of the barbecue grill. Serve hot with your favorite meal.

Makes 4 Servings

nutritional facts
per serving

Calories 51
Total Fat 3g
Cholesterol *trace*
Sodium 1mg
Total Carbohydrate 5g
Dietary Fiber 1g
Protein *trace*

roasted chili and oregano potatoes

Nothing is tastier than seasoned chicken and a side of Roasted Chili and Oregano Potatoes. I often serve these seasoned potatoes with La Jolla Fiesta Chicken (see recipe on page 63).

3 large potatoes, peeled and cut into 8 pieces
2 tablespoons canola oil
1 teaspoon Creole seasoning
1/4 teaspoon salt substitute
1 teaspoon fresh oregano, or 1/8 teaspoon dried oregano
1/2 teaspoon paprika
1/2 teaspoon chili powder
2 tablespoons shredded Romano cheese

Preheat the oven to 350° F. Soak the potatoes in water for 2 minutes. Pat dry and spread out on paper towels for 15 minutes, or until the edges start to harden. Combine all ingredients, except for the potatoes and Romano cheese, in a baking dish, and mix thoroughly. Add the potatoes and stir to coat.

Bake in the oven, uncovered, for 30 minutes. Remove and dust with Romano cheese. Return to oven and bake for 15 more minutes, or until the cheese starts to melt. Serve warm.

Makes 4 Servings

nutritional facts
per serving

Calories 150
Total Fat 8g
Cholesterol 4mg
Sodium 104mg
Total Carbohydrate 17g
Dietary Fiber 2g
Protein 3g

santa fe mashed potatoes

This is not just another boring batch of mashed potatoes—this batch has a delicate southwestern touch. The recipe was inspired by a trip to a little mom and pop restaurant just off the Plaza in Santa Fe. This recipe is great when served as a side dish with Buttermilk Meatloaf (see recipe on page 45).

3 tablespoons Shedd's Spread Country Crock
3 scallions, finely chopped
3 cloves garlic, minced
1/4 cup minced red bell pepper
1/2 cup water
4 medium potatoes, cooked
1/2 teaspoon salt substitute
1/8 teaspoon black pepper

Heat a sauce pan until a drop of water quickly sizzles away. Add 1 tablespoon of the Shedd's Spread, and melt. Add the scallions, garlic, and red bell pepper, and lightly sauté. Cover to keep warm.

In a deep saucepan or large skillet, add the water and bring to a simmer. Add the cooked potatoes and remaining Shedd's Spread, and stir to blend. Add the sautéed ingredients, the salt, and the pepper, and gently blend into the potato mixture. Cook, stirring constantly, until the potatoes start to bubble. Blend well, and serve immediately.

Makes 6-8 Servings

nutritional facts
per serving

Calories 79
Total Fat 2g
Cholesterol *trace*
Sodium 36mg
Total Carbohydrate 15g
Dietary Fiber 1g
Protein 2g

twice cooked white beans

This spicy bean dish has just the right bite. It's a great side dish but can also be a meal in itself. Add a hunk of cornbread for a tasty one-dish supper.

- 1 pound small white beans, washed
- 4 cups Low-Sodium Chicken Stock (see recipe on page 89)
- 4 cups Low-Sodium Beef Stock (see recipe on page 87)
- 1/4 teaspoon black pepper
- 1/2 teaspoon granulated garlic
- 1 teaspoon caraway seeds
- 1 small white onion, chopped
- 1/2 cup imitation bacon bits
- 1 (28-ounce) can tomatoes with green chiles, mild flavored
- 1/2 cup tortilla chips, crumbled
- 2 puff pastry sheets

In a stew pot, combine the beans, chicken stock, and beef stock. Bring to a boil, cover, reduce to a simmer, and cook for 1 hour. Add all remaining ingredients, except for the pastry sheets. Cook for 30 minutes, uncovered, stirring occasionally to avoid sticking.

Preheat the oven to 375° F. Transfer the bean mixture to a deep 13 x 9-inch casserole dish. Cover with the puff pastry sheets. Bake the beans for 35 minutes, or until the pastry is nice and golden. Serve immediately.

Makes 6-8 Servings

nutritional facts
per serving

Calories 432
Total Fat 13g
Cholesterol 0mg
Sodium 539mg
Total Carbohydrate 52g
Dietary Fiber 12g
Protein 13g

stocks, sauces, and basics

low-sodium beef stock

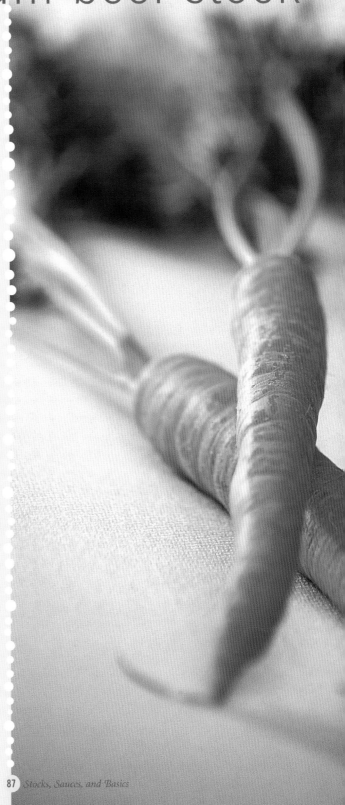

I use this stock to make gravies, as a thickener in hearty stews, and in my competition chili. Keep it handy in the refrigerator.

    4 pounds crosscut beef shank bone,
      cut into 2-inch cubes
    4 cloves garlic, mashed
    2 large carrots, thinly sliced
    2 stalks celery, chopped
    1 large yellow onion, quartered
    3 cups red wine
    3 bay leaves
    4 sprigs fresh parsley
    4 peppercorns, crushed in a mortar
    1/2 teaspoon liquid smoke flavoring
    16 cups water

Preheat the oven to 300° F. In a large roasting pan, combine the bones, garlic, 1 of the sliced carrots, 1 of the celery stalks, and 2 of the onion quarters. Roast for 1/2 hour, turning bones once. Place the hot bones in a deep stew pot. Deglaze the roasting pan by adding the wine and, with a wooden spoon, scrape the bottom. Add deglazed vegetables and juices to stew pot, and follow with remaining ingredients. Bring to a boil and skim the foam. Reduce to a simmer, cover the pot, and cook for 2 hours.

Let the broth cool. Skim off the fat. Remove bones, strain broth, and refrigerate overnight. Skim off the fat after refrigeration. This stock will store in an air-tight container in the refrigerator for up to 2 weeks.

Makes 3 Quarts

nutritional facts
per 1/2 cup

Calories 238
Total Fat 10g
Cholesterol 44mg
Sodium 130mg
Total Carbohydrate 5g
Dietary Fiber 1g
Protein 22g

southwestern-style, low-sodium vegetable stock

This spicy broth can be used as a consommé, a gravy, or a stock. I like to make rice and chicken soup with this flavorful stock.

6 sprigs fresh cilantro, or 1 teaspoon dried cilantro

3 sprigs fresh parsley, or $1/2$ teaspoon dried parsley

2 slices tomato, chopped and drained

1 white onion, sliced $1/4$-inch thick

3 carrots, chopped

3 stalks celery, chopped

1 small green bell pepper, chopped

1 serrano chile, chopped

3 tablespoons extra virgin olive oil

3 quarts water

1 bay leaf

$1/2$ teaspoon chili powder

4 peppercorns, crushed in a mortar

$1/8$ teaspoon coriander seeds, crushed in a mortar

$1/4$ teaspoon mesquite flavoring, optional

1 teaspoon salt substitute

2 teaspoons balsamic vinegar

Dash red pepper flakes

Preheat the oven to 375° F. Combine the cilantro, parsley, all the vegetables, and the olive oil in a deep bowl. Mix well to coat. Spread evenly on a baking sheet. Bake for 30 minutes, or until browned.

Add the water to a stew pot. Add all ingredients, including the baked vegetables. Bring to a boil. Reduce to a simmer, cover, and cook for 1 hour. Remove cover and let simmer for 45 minutes more, or until reduced by about one-fourth. Let cool slightly, and then use in soup or in your choice of a dish. Refrigerate for up to 2 weeks in an air-tight container.

Makes about 2 $1/2$ Quarts

nutritional facts
per $1/2$ cup

Calories 41
Total Fat 3g
Cholesterol *trace*
Sodium 21mg
Total Carbohydrate 4g
Dietary Fiber 1g
Protein 1g

low-sodium chicken stock

I save all my leftover poultry pieces, cooked or uncooked, to make this stock. You will find this stock used in many recipes, including Chile Verde, Macaroni Salad Mexicana, Twice Cooked White Beans, and many others.

    1 (4-pound) stewing chicken, cut up
    4 cloves garlic, minced
    2 large carrots, chopped
    1 stalk celery, chopped
    1 green bell pepper, chopped
    1 large onion, chopped
    8 cloves
    3 bay leaves
    4 stalks parsley
    1 cinnamon stick
    4 peppercorns, crushed in a mortar
    1 1/2 quarts water

Wash the chicken pieces, including giblets, and place in a deep stockpot. Add the remaining ingredients. Bring to a boil, and skim off foam, being careful to leave parsley stems in the stew pot. Reduce to a simmer, cover the pot, and cook for 45 minutes, or until chicken is tender.

Let broth cool at room temperature. Skim off fat. Remove skin, meat, and bones from broth and discard. Strain broth and discard vegetable remains. Refrigerate overnight. Skim off fat that coagulates while refrigerated. Serve in any recipe that calls for a good chicken stock. This stock will store in an air-tight container in the refrigerator for up to 2 weeks.

Makes about 1 Quart

nutritional facts
per 1/2 cup

Calories 53
Total Fat 1g
Cholesterol 17mg
Sodium 34mg
Total Carbohydrate 4g
Dietary Fiber 2g
Protein 7g

texas jack's seasoning

Texas Jack Crowley gave me this muy bueno seasoning a few years back. I added salt substitute and kicked up the spice mix a little. I use it as a dry marinade and add it to my Bronco Beans on page 74. I've also been known to spice up a tall glass of tomato juice with a dab of this zesty blend.

    3 tablespoons chili powder
    1 tablespoon ground cumin
    2 tablespoons red pepper flakes
    2 teaspoons salt substitute
    1 tablespoon Colman's English Mustard powder
    1 teaspoon white pepper
    1 teaspoon granulated garlic
    1 teaspoon dried cilantro, the Mexican
      variety preferred
    1 tablespoon dried oregano, the Mexican
      variety preferred
    1/2 teaspoon jalapeño chile powder
    1 teaspoon celery seeds
    2 tablespoons dried onions
    2 tablespoons paprika

Combine all ingredients in a deep bowl and mix thoroughly. Serve immediately over your favorite dish. Store the excess in an air-tight container in a cool, dry place.

Makes about 1 Cup

nutritional facts
per tablespoon

Calories 23
Total Fat 1g
Cholesterol *trace*
Sodium 21mg
Total Carbohydrate 4g
Dietary Fiber 1g
Protein 1g

cilantro-cumin sauce

Use this sauce as a spicy mix for salad dressings, as a marinade for grilled meat, or as a base for soup. It is also perfect as an extra special flavor in my Chile Verde (see recipe on page 25).

1/2 cup fresh cilantro leaves, tightly packed
1 teaspoon ground cumin
1/4 teaspoon salt substitute
1/2 tablespoon arrowroot
1 tablespoon canola oil
1/4 cup water

Combine all ingredients in a blender and purée. Refrigerate for at least 1 hour before serving.

Makes about 1 Cup

nutritional facts
per 1/2 tablespoon

Calories 9
Total Fat 1g
Cholesterol *trace*
Sodium *trace*
Total Carbohydrate *trace*
Dietary Fiber *trace*
Protein *trace*

hot august night barbecue sauce

This is a quick and easy sauce for ribs or chicken. Slather some on your entrée about 5 minutes before serving. It might be a good idea to triple the recipe so you will have some extra sauce available for other uses.

1/2 cup tomato sauce
1/2 cup apple juice
2 tablespoons chili powder (the hotter the better!)
1 tablespoon honey
2 tablespoons brandy
1/4 teaspoon garlic powder

Combine all ingredients in a skillet. Bring to a boil. Reduce to a simmer and let cook for 15 minutes, stirring occasionally. Let cool slightly before serving. This sauce will keep for up to 2 weeks in an air-tight container in the refrigerator.

Makes about 1 1/4 Cups

nutritional facts
per tablespoon

Calories 46
Total Fat *trace*
Cholesterol *0mg*
Sodium *150mg*
Total Carbohydrate *8g*
Dietary Fiber *1g*
Protein *1g*

dilled champagne sauce

Serve this gourmet sauce hot over angel hair pasta or cold over a fresh garden salad.

1 cup Low-Sodium Chicken Stock (see recipe on page 89)
4 ounces cream cheese, at room temperature
1/2 cup low-fat mayonnaise
2 tablespoons catsup
1 tablespoon cider vinegar
1 teaspoon hot sauce
1/2 cup champagne
2 scallions, minced
1 stalk celery, chopped
3 sprigs fresh dill weed, chopped
2 teaspoons chopped fresh basil
3/4 cup egg substitute, hard-cooked and chopped
1/4 teaspoon salt substitute

Combine all ingredients in a deep sauce pan. Bring to a simmer and stir to blend. Cover and simmer for 10 minutes. Allow to cool slightly before serving.

Makes 3 Cups

nutritional facts
per 1/2 cup

Calories 267
Total Fat 25g
Cholesterol 133mg
Sodium 363mg
Total Carbohydrate 4g
Dietary Fiber *trace*
Protein 7g

dilled parmesan sauce

This cheesy sauce is perfect over steamed vegetables, grilled chicken breasts, or grilled salmon steaks.

2 cups dry white wine
1 tablespoon balsamic vinegar
1 teaspoon honey
3/4 cup shredded Parmesan cheese
1/4 teaspoon celery seeds
1/4 teaspoon dill weed
1 tablespoon Shedd's Spread Country Crock
1/2 cup low-fat evaporated milk
Dash salt substitute
Dash white pepper

Combine all ingredients in a sauce pan and bring to a simmer, stirring often. Let simmer for 5 minutes. Remove from the stove, allow to cool to room temperature, and serve.

Makes about 4 Cups

nutritional facts
per 1/2 cup

Calories 95
Total Fat 3g
Cholesterol 6mg
Sodium 171mg
Total Carbohydrate 3g
Dietary Fiber *trace*
Protein 4g

five flavors sauce

This versatile sauce can be used as a salad dressing or as a sauce over fish, chicken breasts, or medallions of beef. It also makes a great dip for crackers, potato chips, or corn chips. Be creative!

1/4 cup minced scallions
1/4 cup minced red bell pepper
1/4 cup minced green bell pepper
1/4 cup chopped green chiles
1/4 cup minced red onion
1 cup chopped fresh cilantro
1/2 cup low-fat cottage cheese
1/4 cup Mock Sour Cream (see recipe on page 97)
2 tablespoons shredded Parmesan cheese
1 tablespoon canola oil
1/8 teaspoon granulated garlic
1/8 teaspoon salt substitute
1/4 teaspoon hot sauce

Combine all ingredients in a food processor and blend to a creamy finish, about 1 to 1 1/2 minutes. Cover and refrigerate for 1 hour or overnight for the best flavor. Serve over your choice of entrée or with your favorite appetizer.

Makes about 3 Cups

nutritional facts
per cup

Calories 27
Total Fat 1g
Cholesterol 1mg
Sodium 54mg
Total Carbohydrate 2g
Dietary Fiber *trace*
Protein 2g

scallion-cilantro sauce

This tasty sauce is the perfect complement to serve with fish. See the recipe for Teriyaki Tuna Steaks on page 66 for more ideas.

1/2 cup extra virgin olive oil
1/2 cup dry white wine
2 teaspoons balsamic vinegar
2 scallions, minced
1/4 cup minced fresh cilantro
2 cloves garlic, minced
1/4 cup chopped black olives
1/2 cup thinly sliced mushrooms
Dash white pepper
Salt substitute, to taste

In a skillet, combine the olive oil, wine, and balsamic vinegar. Bring to a simmer and cook for 5 minutes. Add the remaining ingredients. Simmer for 5 to 7 minutes, stirring frequently. Serve hot.

Makes about 1 1/2 Cups

nutritional facts
per tablespoon

Calories 47
Total Fat 5g
Cholesterol 0mg
Sodium 13mg
Total Carbohydrate 1g
Dietary Fiber *trace*
Protein *trace*

nutmeg butter sauce

This slightly sweet sauce can be served over pork or chicken, or brush a generous teaspoon on top of a steak just before it comes off the grill. It also goes well over your favorite pasta.

- 1/4 cup Shedd's Spread Country Crock, melted
- 1 cup low-fat evaporated milk
- 1/4 cup minced red bell pepper
- 1/2 cup minced red onion
- 1/4 teaspoon crushed nutmeg
- 1/4 teaspoon Colman's English Mustard powder
- Dash white pepper
- Salt substitute, to taste

Add all ingredients to a saucepan. Bring to a simmer and let cook, stirring often, for 15 minutes. Immediately pour over your entrée.

Makes about 1 Cup

nutritional facts
per tablespoon

Calories 25
Total Fat 1g
Cholesterol 1mg
Sodium 139mg
Total Carbohydrate 2g
Dietary Fiber *trace*
Protein 1g

plata sonora sauce

I use this Plata Sonora Sauce on chicken breasts and on my homemade Spiced Veal Meatballs (see recipe on page 52).

- 1/4 cup catsup
- 1 cup Mock Sour Cream (see recipe on page 97)
- 1/2 cup low-fat mayonnaise
- 1/4 cup minced capers
- 1 teaspoon lime juice
- 1/4 cup tequila
- 1/4 teaspoon salt substitute

Combine all ingredients in a bowl and blend thoroughly. Serve immediately. This sauce can be stored in the refrigerator for up to 2 weeks in an air-tight container.

Makes about 2 1/4 Cups

nutritional facts
per tablespoon

Calories 25
Total Fat 1g
Cholesterol 2mg
Sodium 99mg
Total Carbohydrate 1g
Dietary Fiber *trace*
Protein 2g

spicy tomato sauce

Add this tasty sauce to some jasmine rice and cooked shrimp, and you've got a special meal. It's a dandy of a sauce to have around to serve with all sorts of entrées.

1/2 cup minced white onion
1 clove garlic, minced
6 chopped plum tomatoes
2 tablespoons tomato paste
1/2 teaspoon white pepper
1/2 teaspoon dried oregano, the Mexican variety preferred
1 serrano chile, minced
1 tablespoon minced fresh cilantro

Add all ingredients to a blender, and purée. In a skillet, bring all blended ingredients to a simmer. Let simmer, stirring often, until the liquid starts to thicken. Serve immediately. This sauce can be refrigerated in an air-tight container for up to 2 weeks.

Makes about 2 Cups

nutritional facts
per tablespoon

Calories 10
Total Fat *trace*
Cholesterol 0*mg*
Sodium 19*mg*
Total Carbohydrate 2*g*
Dietary Fiber *trace*
Protein *trace*

tomatillos, chile, and cumin sauce

This is a great basic sauce for a variety of foods. I often use it to enhance my competition-winning Chile Verde (see recipe on page 25) and as a sauce for enchiladas.

10 tomatillos, shucked, cleaned, and quartered
1 medium white onion, chopped
1/2 teaspoon ground cumin
1/2 teaspoon mild chili powder
1/8 teaspoon salt substitute
1 (4-ounce) can diced green chiles
1/4 cup water
1/4 cup canola oil

Combine all ingredients in a blender and reduce to a pulp. Cover and refrigerate for at least 1 hour to allow the flavors to blend. Add to a big bowl of Chile Verde or across the top of a batch of homemade enchiladas. This sauce will keep in an air-tight container in the refrigerator for up to 2 weeks.

Makes about 1 Quart

nutritional facts
per tablespoon

Calories 21
Total Fat 2*g*
Cholesterol *trace*
Sodium 1*mg*
Total Carbohydrate 1*g*
Dietary Fiber *trace*
Protein *trace*

cilantro powder

Cilantro Powder is used as an ingredient in sauces and salad dressings. I mix it with olive oil and spread it on grilled pork chops or grilled fish just prior to serving.

> 1/2 pound fresh cilantro, about 3
>   large bunches
> 1/2 teaspoon garlic powder

Wash the cilantro in cold water. Remove any wilting stems. Gently dry with a paper towel.

Preheat the oven to 150° F., or minimum heat. Arrange the cilantro in a single layer on a cookie sheet, and bake for 4 to 6 hours, or until completely dry.

In a dry blender or food processor, grind the dried cilantro until it is a powder. Pour into a mixing bowl, add the garlic powder, and mix thoroughly. Add to your favorite dish. Store the excess in an air-tight container in a cool, dry place.

Makes about ½ Cup

nutritional facts
per tablespoon

Calories 13
Total Fat *trace*
Cholesterol 0*mg*
Sodium 10*mg*
Total Carbohydrate 2*g*
Dietary Fiber *trace*
Protein 1*g*

ginger and orange chicken marinade

I use this recipe when I am going to grill chicken breasts. First, I marinate the chicken, and second, while it cooks, I baste the chicken with the same marinade. These flavors also work very well on pork chops and sea bass.

> 1 cup orange juice
> 1 tablespoon canola oil
> 1 teaspoon finely minced ginger root
> 1/2 teaspoon El Pato hot sauce, or your
>   favorite brand
> 1/2 teaspoon garlic powder
> 1/4 teaspoon salt substitute

Mix all ingredients together in a medium bowl. Pour over the chicken breasts and turn until well coated. Refrigerate and marinate for at least 2 hours. Smoke, grill, or bake your chicken, and brush more marinade on the breasts as they cook. Serve hot off the grill.

Makes about 1 Cup

nutritional facts
per tablespoon

Calories 15
Total Fat 1*g*
Cholesterol *trace*
Sodium 2*mg*
Total Carbohydrate 2*g*
Dietary Fiber *trace*
Protein *trace*

hatch chile paste

Hatch Chile Paste is best used to add spicy flavor to anything that needs a little kick such as sauces, soups, or marinades. Be cautious, though, because it can pack a wallop if you use a hot chile. For the best low-key results, I suggest you use mild New Mexico, Anaheim chiles, or green Pasilla chiles.

4 cups roasted and peeled New Mexico
   green chiles
4 tablespoons extra virgin olive oil
1/2 teaspoon garlic powder
1/2 teaspoon onion powder
1/4 teaspoon ground cumin
1/4 teaspoon salt substitute

Remove the seeds and veins from the chiles. Add the chiles and other ingredients to a blender or food processor and purée. Add to any dish that requires some spicing up.

    Place the extra paste in an air-tight container and cover with a thin layer of olive oil to preserve. Keep in the refrigerator for up to 2 weeks.

Makes about 4 Cups

nutritional facts
per tablespoon

Calories 17
Total Fat 1g
Cholesterol *trace*
Sodium 2mg
Total Carbohydrate 2g
Dietary Fiber *trace*
Protein *trace*

jaime's serious chile seasoning

This seasoning is meaner than an old bull and should be used sparingly. You can use it creatively in dishes that need some serious seasoning.

2 serrano chiles, chopped
1 jalapeño chile, chopped
3 teaspoons pickled jalapeño, with juice
1 teaspoon chile de arbol powder, or
   chili powder
1 habanero chile
2 tablespoons arrowroot powder
1 teaspoon white pepper
2 teaspoons masa corn flour
1 cup Mexican beer
1 teaspoon fresh lime juice
1/2 teaspoon Splenda sugar substitute
1/2 teaspoon salt substitute

Combine all ingredients in a blender and blend thoroughly. Add to a sauce pan and simmer for 10 minutes. Allow to cool slightly and add it to your favorite dish. Refrigerate the excess in an air-tight container for up to 1 month.

Makes about 2 Cups

nutritional facts
per tablespoon

Calories 5
Total Fat *trace*
Cholesterol *trace*
Sodium 5mg
Total Carbohydrate 1g
Dietary Fiber *trace*
Protein *trace*

mock sour cream

This sour cream recipe is a mainstay in a lot of my recipes. You can use it on almost all southwestern dishes, and it is a breeze to make. If you want to add more flavor, you can use any of your favorite herbs or spices.

> 2 cups low-fat cottage cheese
> 1/2 cup low-fat buttermilk

Combine the ingredients in a blender and process until smooth, scraping down the sides of the blender often. Add a dollop to the top of any dish, especially the spicy ones. Refrigerate the excess in an air-tight container for up to 2 weeks.

Makes 2 1/2 Cups

nutritional facts
per tablespoon

Calories 9
Total Fat *trace*
Cholesterol 1*mg*
Sodium 149*mg*
Total Carbohydrate *trace*
Dietary Fiber 0*g*
Protein 1*g*

parmesan el rico

This spicy Parmesan mix is great on pasta dishes and is a prime ingredient in La Jolla Fiesta Chicken (see recipe on page 63).

> 1 cup shredded Parmesan cheese
> 1 teaspoon chili powder
> 1/8 teaspoon cayenne
> 1 tablespoon minced fresh cilantro

Preheat the oven to 350° F. Thoroughly combine all ingredients in an ovenproof container. Bake for 15 to 20 minutes, or until the cheese is golden brown. Serve over any dish that needs a little more flavor.

Makes 1 Cup

nutritional facts
per tablespoon

Calories 24
Total Fat 2*g*
Cholesterol 4*mg*
Sodium 95*mg*
Total Carbohydrate *trace*
Dietary Fiber *trace*
Protein 2*g*

baked goods

seasoned bread crumbs

This easy-to-make recipe has a thousand uses. Consider using it as a seasoned layer over baked clams, as a topping over a salad, or as a tasty addition to a quart of gazpacho. It can also be added to a spinach and cream cheese mixture and then stuffed in large pasta shells.

4 cups bread crumbs, any type
1 teaspoon salt substitute
1/2 teaspoon minced fresh oregano
1/2 teaspoon minced fresh basil
1 teaspoon minced garlic
1/2 teaspoon onion powder
1 teaspoon tarragon
1 1/2 teaspoons sesame seeds
1 tablespoon olive oil

Preheat the oven to 325° F. In a deep bowl, combine all ingredients, except for the olive oil, and mix thoroughly. Spread evenly across a baking sheet, and bake for 15 minutes, stirring every five minutes. Let cool. Add to a deep bowl or mixer bowl, and hand-blend or mix on low speed. Add the olive oil in slow drizzles to blend. Use in your favorite dish. Refrigerate any extra crumbs in an air-tight container for up to 2 weeks.

Makes Approximately 4 Cups, about 36 Servings

nutritional facts
per tablespoon

Calories 58
Total Fat 1g
Cholesterol trace
Sodium 116mg
Total Carbohydrate 10g
Dietary Fiber trace
Protein 2g

little corn tortillas

Little tortillas have so many uses from mini-tacos to personal-size quesadillas to tapas. With this recipe you can make your own Little Corn Tortillas, and believe me, when you make them yourself, they are so much better than the store-bought varieties.

For a little variation, create red tortillas by adding 3 table-spoons of ketchup to the mixing bowl and reducing the vegetable stock by the same amount. Or, for green tortillas, add 4 table-spoons of cilantro powder and 2 drops of green food coloring but do not reduce the stock.

2 cups masa corn flour
1/2 teaspoon granulated garlic
1/4 teaspoon cayenne
1/2 teaspoon salt substitute
1 1/3 cups Low-Sodium Vegetable Stock
(see recipe on page 88)

In a mixing bowl, combine the masa, garlic, cayenne, and salt, and blend thoroughly. Add the vegetable stock in small quantities and blend until a consistent dough ball forms. Wrap the dough in plastic wrap and refrigerate for 30 minutes.

Form the dough into 36 equal portions. Flatten them with the bottom of a salad plate, a tamale press, or a dough roller. Heat up a griddle and cook the tortillas, a few at a time, for 3 to 5 minutes per side, or until small brown baking spots appear. Serve warm.

Makes about 36 Little Tortillas, about 18 Servings

nutritional facts
per serving

Calories 22
Total Fat *trace*
Cholesterol *trace*
Sodium 45mg
Total Carbohydrate 4g
Dietary Fiber *trace*
Protein 1g

bandito bolillos

If you have ever been to a Mexican bakery or market, you will find a tasty dinner roll called a bolillo. I have a fond affection for these delectable morsels and have worked hard to perfect my own version of the recipe. It took several test runs and a chat with my favorite Mexican baker before I learned the trick (psst, it's the cinnamon—but keep that our secret). So bake up a batch of these wonderful rolls and, while they are still hot, fill them with your favorite carb-smart preserve.

2 1/2 cups warm water
2 tablespoons dry yeast
2 1/2 teaspoons Splenda sugar substitute
4 cups all-purpose flour
1 cup cornmeal
1/2 cup powdered milk
1/2 teaspoon ground cinnamon
1 tablespoon salt substitute
2 teaspoons baking powder
2 teaspoons canola oil

Heat 1 cup of the water to about 110° F., approximately 15 seconds in a microwave. Add the yeast and 1/2 teaspoon of the Splenda to the warm water. Stir to mix and let stand for 10 minutes until bubbly.

In a large bowl, combine the yeast mixture, remaining water and 2 cups of the all-purpose flour. Mix to form a sticky dough. Set aside for 30 minutes in a warm place (I use a barely warm oven). Stir in the cornmeal, powdered milk, remaining Splenda, cinnamon, salt substitute, baking powder, and canola oil; mix thoroughly. Add the remaining flour, 1/2 cup at a time, to form a dough ball.

Place the dough on a lightly-floured bread board, sprinkle more flour on top of the dough, and knead for 10 minutes, adding more flour if necessary. Spray the dough ball with vegetable oil and return to the bowl. Let rise until doubled in size, about 1 hour.

Preheat the oven to 375° F. Punch dough down, form into 12 small oblong rolls about 4-inches long, and twist the ends. Place on a baking sheet dusted with cornmeal. Let rise about 30 minutes, or until doubled.

Bake in the oven for 10 minutes. Reduce oven temperature to 350° F. and bake for 30 minutes more, or until golden brown.

Makes 10-12 Bolillos, about 10 Servings

nutritional facts
per serving

Calories 191
Total Fat 3g
Cholesterol 5mg
Sodium 104mg
Total Carbohydrate 40g
Dietary Fiber 2g
Protein 6g

fiesta jalapeño cornbread muffinettes

These mini-rolls are the perfect accompaniment to my Chile Verde (see recipe on page 25). For a nifty snack, serve these little muffins hot with jalapeño jelly or honey and a dab of fresh butter.

2 cups low-fat milk

1/2 cup egg substitute

1 medium jalapeño chile, minced

1 teaspoon ground cumin

1 cup masa corn flour

1 cup all-purpose flour

1 cup white cornmeal or yellow cornmeal

3 tablespoons Splenda sugar substitute

2 tablespoons baking powder

1/2 cup minced red bell pepper

1 cup coarsely chopped green chile

1 medium red onion, coarsely chopped

1/2 teaspoon granulated garlic

1/4 cup minced cilantro

1/4 teaspoon salt substitute

1/2 cup canola oil

Combine the milk, egg substitute, jalapeño, and cumin in a blender and mix for 25 to 30 seconds. Add the milk mix and remaining ingredients to a mixing bowl, and mix thoroughly.

Preheat the oven to 400° F. Spray 3 mini muffin pans with non-stick cooking spray. Spoon the mix into the pans, about 2 teaspoons per section. Bake for 25 minutes, or until a toothpick inserted in the middle of a muffin comes out clean. Remove from the pan, and serve warm.

Makes 30 Muffinettes, about 30 Servings

nutritional facts
per serving

Calories 117
Total Fat 6g
Cholesterol 1mg
Sodium 140mg
Total Carbohydrate 15g
Dietary Fiber 1g
Protein 4g

focaccia with a southwestern twist

This unique focaccia bread is a great palate pleaser, and it is an appetizer that will have your guests begging for the recipe. I serve the focaccia with a couple of different salsas for dipping.

1/2 teaspoon Splenda sugar substitute

1/4 ounce dry yeast

1 cup warm water

2 cups all-purpose flour

3/4 cup yellow cornmeal

1 teaspoon salt substitute

3/4 cup minced chorizo

1 (4-ounce) can diced green chile

1 cup cubed mozzarella cheese

2 tablespoons olive oil

1/4 cup shredded Parmesan cheese

Preheat the oven to 400° F. In a warm measuring cup combine the sugar, yeast, and water. Let stand for about ten minutes until frothy. In a deep mixing bowl, add the flour, cornmeal, salt, chorizo, chiles, mozzarella cheese, and olive oil. Add the yeast blend to the flour mixture and mix thoroughly.

Roll out on a floured breadboard, sprinkle the dough with more flour, and then knead until the stickiness is gone, adding more flour as needed. Place in a greased bowl, roll to coat, and let stand for 10 minutes. Spray a 10 x 15-inch cookie sheet with non-stick cooking spray. Roll out the dough on the sheet, and spread out so that it completely covers the sheet, making sure to press the dough into the corners. Brush the dough with olive oil and sprinkle with Parmesan.

Bake for 20 minutes, or until the top is golden brown. Remove from the oven to cool. Cut into 24 squares and serve.

Makes 24 Servings

nutritional facts
per serving

Calories 118
Total Fat 6g
Cholesterol 11mg
Sodium 127mg
Total Carbohydrate 12g
Dietary Fiber 1g
Protein 5g

garlic & herb toasted bread slices

Here's another quick and easy appetizer. I serve this popular recipe at brunches and parties.

4 tablespoons olive oil
2 tablespoons shredded Romano cheese
1/2 teaspoon crushed coriander seeds
1/2 teaspoon dried oregano, the Mexican variety preferred
1/2 teaspoon onion powder
1/4 teaspoon garlic powder
1/2 teaspoon Old Bay Seasoning
8 slices French bread

Preheat the oven to 375° F. In a small bowl, combine all ingredients except for the bread. Spread over the bread slices. Form the slices into a loaf and wrap in aluminum foil. Bake for 20 minutes. Remove from the oven and serve hot as an appetizer or with your favorite meal.

Makes 8 Servings

nutritional facts
per serving

Calories 68
Total Fat 7g
Cholesterol 2mg
Sodium 61mg
Total Carbohydrate trace
Dietary Fiber trace
Protein 1g

vaquero bizcocho

I like these Cowboy Biscuits hot from the oven. For a spicy treat, stir some chopped up jalapeños into the dough mix. You'll be amazed at the blend of flavors in these delicious biscuits.

1 cup self-rising flour
1/2 cup cornmeal
1/2 cup egg substitute
1/4 cup strong coffee (like Sumatra or French roast)
1/2 cup low-fat milk
1 tablespoon canola oil
1/8 teaspoon Splenda sugar substitute
1/2 teaspoon baking powder
1/8 teaspoon baking soda
Pinch salt substitute

Preheat the oven to 400° F. Mix all ingredients together in a deep bowl and let stand for 15 minutes. Spoon the mix into muffin tins, about 1 tablespoon per section. Bake for 15 minutes. Test for doneness by sticking a wooden toothpick into a biscuit. If it comes out wet then bake the biscuits for 2 to 3 minutes longer. Serve with your favorite meal.

Makes 12 Biscuits, about 12 Servings

nutritional facts
per serving

Calories 88
Total Fat 3g
Cholesterol 1mg
Sodium 191mg
Total Carbohydrate 13g
Dietary Fiber 1g
Protein 3g

desserts

pumpkin and cherry pudding

Everyone enjoys the flavor of a good pumpkin pie. Well, add this recipe to your list of ways to serve pumpkin. This nifty pudding is a winner.

- 1 (14-ounce) can pumpkin
- 2 (1 1/2-ounce) packages sugar-free Jell-O vanilla pudding mix
- 1 cup pitted and minced cherries
- 1 cup Splenda sugar substitute
- 1/2 teaspoon salt substitute
- 1/2 teaspoon nutmeg, or cinnamon
- 1/2 teaspoon ground ginger
- 3/4 cup egg substitute
- 2/3 cup low-fat evaporated milk
- 1 1/2 cups low-fat milk

Preheat the oven to 400° F. In a deep mixing bowl, add all ingredients. Blend thoroughly. Pour into 6 ovenproof serving bowls. Bake for 45 minutes. Remove from the oven when a knife inserted into the middle comes out clean. Allow to cool. Serve as is or top off with light whipped cream.

Makes 6 Servings

nutritional facts
per serving

Calories 126
Total Fat 4g
Cholesterol 4mg
Sodium 137mg
Total Carbohydrate 82g
Dietary Fiber 2g
Protein 9g

strawberry and pineapple meringue

Here's a dessert with many flavors. You can use all kinds of fruit in this recipe, including finely minced tangerines, oranges, or mashed bananas with coconut. Make sure you use a brand of egg substitute like Egg Beaters, which is pasteurized making it safe in recipes calling for uncooked eggs.

1/2 cup pineapple juice
1 cup egg substitute
1 cup Splenda sugar substitute
1 cup fresh strawberries
Extra strawberries
Fresh mint sprigs

Put 2 tablespoons of pineapple juice in each of the wine glasses or custard cups. Keep them in the freezer until frozen solid.

In a large mixing bowl add the egg substitute, Splenda, and 1 cup of the strawberries. Beat on high speed for about 4 to 5 minutes, or until firm. Spoon on top of the frozen pineapple juice. Garnish with extra strawberries and fresh mint. Serve immediately.

Makes 6 Servings

nutritional facts
per serving

Calories 62
Total Fat 3g
Cholesterol 1mg
Sodium 60mg
Total Carbohydrate 58g
Dietary Fiber trace
Protein 4g

plátanos de chocolate

This delicious recipe for chocolate-covered bananas is simple and will satisfy anyone in the sweet tooth crowd.

4 large bananas
1 tablespoon Shedd's Spread Country Crock
1 cup chocolate-coated peanuts
8 teaspoons Mock Sour Cream (see recipe on page 97)
8 sprigs fresh spearmint

Slice the bananas lengthwise then halve them again to make 16 quarters. Heat a skillet until a drop of water quickly sizzles away. Add the Shedd's Spread and swirl to coat the skillet. Add the bananas and fry for 1 minute on each side, or until they are just starting to brown. Remove and drain on paper towels.

Place two banana quarters in eight small desert dishes. Spoon equal amounts of chocolate-coated peanuts over each set of bananas. Add a teaspoon of Mock Sour Cream to each and garnish with spearmint sprigs.

Makes 8 Servings

nutritional facts
per serving

Calories 200
Total Fat 7g
Cholesterol 5mg
Sodium 268mg
Total Carbohydrate 25g
Dietary Fiber 3g
Protein 11g

taos toasted oatmeal cookies

These scrumptious morsels will be a mainstay in your cookie jar.

3 cups instant oatmeal
3/4 cup Splenda sugar substitute
3/4 cup canola oil
3 tablespoons egg substitute
1 1/2 teaspoons vanilla extract
2 tablespoons dark molasses
4 tablespoons water
1 1/2 cups all-purpose flour
1/2 teaspoon cinnamon
1/2 teaspoon salt substitute
1 teaspoon baking soda
1 1/2 cups low-fat milk

Preheat the oven to 350° F. Spread the oatmeal on a cookie sheet and toast in the oven for 20 minutes, turning once.

In a greased bowl, combine the remaining ingredients. Add the oatmeal and mix until it forms a soft dough. Spray a cookie sheet with vegetable spray and place 16 little dabs (1 teaspoon each) of cookie dough on the sheet. Bake for 15 minutes, or until lightly browned. Remove and let cool for 5 minutes before serving.

Makes about 60 Cookies

nutritional facts
per cookie

Calories 55
Total Fat 3g
Cholesterol *trace*
Sodium 65mg
Total Carbohydrate 11g
Dietary Fiber 1g
Protein 1g

baja-style baked rice pudding

This recipe is similar to one I had at a little bed and breakfast in Cabo San Lucas. To make this pudding even more special, try presoaking the raisins in 1 tablespoon of rum until they absorb all the liquid, adding 1 teaspoon of lime or orange zest to the casserole dish before baking, or sprinkling 1/4 cup of grated coconut on the top of the pudding after the first 30 minutes of baking when the foil has been removed. Ah, the flavors of Mexico!

1 cup long grain white rice

2 1/2 cups low-fat milk

1/2 cup low-fat evaporated milk

1 teaspoon vanilla extract

1/4 teaspoon finely ground cardamom

1/2 teaspoon cinnamon

1/4 cup egg substitute

3/4 cup raisins

2 tablespoons Shedd's Spread Country Crock

1/4 cup Splenda sugar substitute

Bring a large pot of water to a brisk boil, add the rice, and cook for 8 minutes. Rinse under cold water to stop the cooking process and drain.

Preheat the oven to 350° F. In a deep skillet, combine the milk, evaporated milk, vanilla extract, cardamom, and cinnamon. Bring mixture to a boil, stirring often. Remove from heat and stir in the egg substitute, raisins, Shedd's Spread, and Splenda. Let mixture cool for 15 minutes.

Add all ingredients, including the rice, to an 8 x 8-inch casserole dish (or a 10-inch quiche dish). Stir to blend. Cover with foil and bake for 30 minutes. Remove the foil and discard. Stir mixture again. Bake for 30 more minutes to form a tasty crust. Serve warm.

Makes 12 Servings

nutritional facts
per serving

Calories 129
Total Fat 2g
Cholesterol 3mg
Sodium 63mg
Total Carbohydrate 32g
Dietary Fiber 1g
Protein 4g

baked bananas magdalena

A small dollop of low-fat vanilla yogurt on the side is a nice complement to this tasty dessert.

> 1 tablespoon Shedd's Spread Country Crock
> 1 teaspoon Splenda sugar substitute
> Dash nutmeg
> 1/4 teaspoon lime juice
> 1 tablespoon light rum
> 2 large bananas, quartered
> 4 sprigs fresh mint

Preheat the oven to 400° F. In a sauté pan, combine the Shedd's Spread, Splenda, nutmeg, lime juice, and rum. Cook over low heat, stirring constantly, until thoroughly melted. Remove from heat.

Place the bananas in a small baking dish. Cover with the liquid mix. Bake for 20 minutes. Garnish each dessert with a fresh mint sprig and serve warm.

Makes 4-6 Servings

nutritional facts
per serving

Calories 75
Total Fat 1g
Cholesterol 0mg
Sodium 22mg
Total Carbohydrate 17g
Dietary Fiber 2g
Protein 1g

west texas peach cobbler

I've made this recipe in a variety of ways. I've baked it in the oven, on a grill, and in a Dutch oven alongside a trout stream. It's a never-fail recipe, especially when you use that old stand-by, Karo syrup.

  1 cup self-rising flour
  1 cup low-fat milk
  1/2 cup Splenda sugar substitute
  2 cups sliced peaches, about 8 peaches
  1/4 cup light Karo syrup
  1 teaspoon ground allspice
  1/2 cup Shedd's Spread Country
    Crock, softened
Light whipping cream

Preheat oven to 350° F. In a deep bowl, mix together the flour, milk, and Splenda. Grease a heavy all-metal skillet or Dutch oven, and add the flour mixture.

In a separate bowl, combine the sliced peaches, Karo syrup, and allspice. Mix well, and add to the flour mixture. Dot with remaining Shedd's Spread. Swirl to blend.

Bake in the oven for 30 to 35 minutes, or until a crumbly crust rises and turns golden brown. Remove from the oven and let cool slightly. Spoon equal portions into bowls and top with a dollop of light whipping cream.

Makes 6 Servings

nutritional facts
per serving

Calories 208
Total Fat 6g
Cholesterol 2mg
Sodium 409mg
Total Carbohydrate 70g
Dietary Fiber 2g
Protein 4g

acknowledgements

This is my third cookbook with Northland Publishing, and it was the hardest of all. Thanks to Tammy Gales-Biber and the other Northland folks. The job was made easier with a well-defined set of manuscript rules (and, no doubt, at the editing end, some patience with my style). For the last ten years, Northland and I have been "partners," and I feel that the next ten will be even better. Thanks partners!

In the quest to create worthy recipes and cookbooks, I need guinea pigs, not for cooking, mind you, but for testing the results of my time at the stove, grill, and cutting board. I refer to these brave souls as piglets, and under most circumstances, they didn't even know they were being used. It was at parties and other gatherings that I slipped them a few new concoctions. As for the head piglet, my wife, Jodi, she suffers with new creations all the time (must be part of marriage). In her case, I stress that she give me her honest opinion about each recipe. When Jodi finds the recipe too spicy, then I know the Southwest chile heat is just about right.

I have to give a special thanks to international boxing commentator and ESPN radio host, Al Bernstein. He's been the victim of several of my attempts to create a unique salsa bearing his name. Well, I finally slapped together a stinger that should do him justice—it's a salsa with a knockout punch. The New Bernstein Salsa is located on page 19.

I would also like to give a hardy tip of the Stetson to my good friend, Pat Hanneman. She graciously carried me past some rough spots on MasterCook 7, the program I used to create recipes and gather nutritional facts found in this book. Gracias, Pat, you saved me from falling into a writer's dungeon.

Last, but by far not the least, I have to wave the Stetson and let out a hardy yee haw to my fellow chile-head and well-known author and editor, Dave DeWitt. Poor Dave had the hassle of doing the foreword on this book. He and I have been keeping in touch ever since he published one of my magazine articles while working as the editor honcho at *Chile Pepper Magazine*. If you want to know about chiles, then purchase a copy of any of his books, especially the epic work *The Pepper Encyclopedia*. It's like a bible to me when it comes to learning about chiles. Thank you!

mail order sources

505 southwestern chile products

5555 Montgomery NE
Albuquerque, NM 80109
888.505.CHILE
www.505chile.com
Red and green salsa (organic and natural),
chile gift kits, and other food products

la tortilla factory

3635 Standish Avenue
Santa Rosa, CA 95407
800.446.1516
www.latortillafactory.com
Low-carb/low-fat tortillas

all things chili

P.O. Box 71015
Las Vegas, NV 89170
702.812.5024
702.924.8586 (fax)
www.allthingschili.com
Chili powders, spices, seeds, canned goods,
cookbooks, apparel, stoves, and gear

santa cruz chili & spice co.

P.O. Box 177
Tumacacori, AZ 85640
520.398.2591
520.398.2592 (fax)
www.santacruzchili.com
Chili paste, chile powder, hot sauces,
and a variety of spices

hatch chile company

P.O. Box 752
Deming, NM 88031
800.359.1483
Canned chiles and other food products

sespe creek chili and spice company

805.524.2078
661.387.9849 (fax)
Chili powders, cumin, oregano,
and other spices

index

index